UNDERWRITING

— ● — ● — ● — ● —

WHAT EVERY PRODUCER MUST KNOW

To Jean
Cheers &
Warm Best Wishes!
always!
Hank

HANK GEORGE, FALU, CLU, FLMI

with a chapter on

FINANCIAL UNDERWRITING

by DUWAYNE KILBO, MBA, FLMI

© HGI Press

Dedication

This book is lovingly dedicated to the HGI
team: Esther, Matthew, Rachel and Rick.

TABLE OF CONTENTS

———•———•———•———•———

FOREWORD

———•——•——•——•———

Life insurance producers (our synonym here for agent, broker and all other genre of insurance salespersons) depend upon accurate and efficient underwriting to get the policies applied for by their clients approved in a way which is conducive to placing the coverage in force. Hence, producers have a vested interest in understanding the risk appraisal process and, by doing so, working in harmony with the home office underwriter to realize this goal.

Life insurance underwriting is undergoing a radical transformation which began nearly two decades ago with the first experiments with what has come to be known as teleunderwriting. This process exerted a transforming effect on every aspect of the risk appraisal process. It has reduced new business acquisition costs as well as application-to-issue cycle time. Its impact in these key domains has catalyzed major changes in the deployment of the risk screening process, forsaking the slower and more costly requirements of the 20th century in favor of expeditious alternatives. Where the producer and his or her client are concerned, this metamorphosis has been a breath of fresh air in terms of their perceptions of underwriting and those who undertake the daunting task of appraising insurability.

The author intuitively knows and steadfastly maintains that our producer-driven life insurance distribution system has always been and shall remain the cornerstone of this industry's success. To that end, this book was written to provide producers with a contemporary understanding of the essential elements driving the underwriting process. To the extent that it contributes to making what we underwriters do transparent and comprehensible to our partners in the field, it will have accomplished its mission.

I would like to thank the many insurance and reinsurance underwriting professionals who shared their thoughts and insights with me in the course of researching and writing this book. It is a regrettable reality of our times that prevailing corporate policies constrain me from mentioning them by name, as they deserve.

I owe a special debt to DuWayne "DK" Kilbo of Windsor Insurance Associates, Inc. for his brilliant chapter on FINANCIAL UNDERWRITING. Given my own shortcomings in this complex domain, this book would have been hopelessly incomplete without his magnificent contribution. DK also peer-reviewed the rest of this book, making valued contributions.

I would also like to thank my longtime friend Dave Wheeler, Senior Vice President and Chief Underwriter for RGA Re, for peer-reviewing this book. Dave made many priceless suggestions, which I eagerly embraced.

The layout and design of **UNDERWRITING: What Every Producer Must Know** is solely the handiwork of beloved daughter Rachel Taylor, Director of Dirk Burton Ltd. and graphic designer for Hank George Inc.

If, at the end of the day, this book makes some small contribution to enhancing the relationship between two of the great professions of our industry – producer and underwriter – then our purpose for writing it will have been richly realized.

Cheers and Peace,

Hank George, FALU, CLU, FLMI
Underwriter

CHAPTER 1

———•———•———•———•———

Underwriting, Underwriters and Producers

What is an underwriter?

An insurance professional accountable for assessing the insurability status of applicants, typically with as little information as possible and under excruciating pressure to make a decision "yesterday."

Where does this excruciating pressure come from?

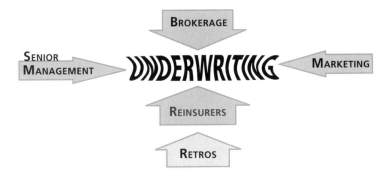

What does each of these compelling forces want from underwriting?

PRODUCERS want it done as liberally as possible…"yesterday."

REINSURERS and their retrocessionaires (reinsurers who reinsure reinsurers) want it done as conservatively as possible…whenever.

MARKETING wants it done in whatever way brings in the most new business.

SENIOR MANAGEMENT wants it done as profitably as possible…and "yesterday"…and on a beer budget!

What does the underwriter want?

An aspirin.

Is underwriting a profession?

Absolutely.

We have the professional designation Fellow of the Academy of Life Underwriting (FALU) which an underwriter earns through a defined course of study. We also have a quarterly journal, *On The Risk*.

The national Association of Home Office Underwriters (AHOU) has over 1,000 members plus there's a regional, state and local network of over 25 smaller associations.

However, one cannot earn an academic degree in underwriting, and thus professional underwriters come from all fields of study and do most of their learning "on the job."

Has underwriting changed over the last few decades?

ENORMOUSLY…and the pace of change is accelerating.

The year I became an underwriter (1973), one might have rightly described the home office underwriter as living in an ivory tower, applying arbitrary rules made and enforced by doctors.

Today, the ivory towers are gone, the rules have become "guidelines" and the doctors now provide technical medical opinions which the underwriter may (or may not) choose to embrace.

What is the primary job responsibility of a professional underwriter?

To sort individual risks into six broad risk categories, based on the evidence gathered during the risk appraisal process.

Insured	Not Insured
Preferred	Postponed
Standard	Declined
Substandard (Rated)	File Closed

What does "substandard" mean?

The applicant can be insured but not at preferred or standard premium rates.

Substandard risks are handled in one of three ways:

- Table rating based on % extra mortality risk
- Flat extra charge expressed in dollars per thousand of coverage for certain medical risks and most non-medical risks
- Exclusion rider, mainly for aviation activities in life insurance and many medical conditions in disability and health insurance

How important is underwriting to insurers?

There are three main sources of insurer profitability: expense savings, investment yields and mortality gains.

Right now, mortality gains loom large as the driver of profitability.

Actuaries set the prices based on reasonable expectations, but it is the underwriters, in their day-to-day handling of your business, who ultimately determine which side of the ledger is impacted by insurers' actual-to-expected mortality.

How important is underwriting to producers?

In the November 2007 issue of *Life Insurance Marketing*, there was a bar chart showing what producers find to be "the most challenging aspects of selling insurance."

Nine factors were ranked. Four of them related directly to underwriting!

Ranking	Factor
2	Getting a policy issued
5	Getting coverage on clients with health problems
7	Application length and complexity
9	Overall home office support

Does underwriting relate directly to producers' success?

You bet it does.

In the 2004 LIMRA International study "Insights into Strengthening Producer Relationships" by Denise C. Marvell, CLU, ChFC, FLMI, ACS, "good home office support" and "fast and competitive underwriting" ranked second and third, respectively, behind "good sales and marketing support."

How many "kinds" of underwriters are there?

It depends on your term of reference. One can classify them by employer, product line, work venue or level of authority.

What are brokerage agency underwriters?

Underwriters employed by brokerage agencies to prepare cases for submission to insurers and facilitate their placement on the most favorable basis possible.

A good friend who is a brokerage agency underwriter describes his work as "underwriting advocacy," which nicely sums it up.

I used to tease these folks, saying they'd crossed over to the "dark side"...

...but the plain truth is that they play a crucial role in the process of getting new business issued and placed on a competitive basis.

And I might add that some of the finest technical underwriting experts I have ever known (DuWayne "DK" Kilbo, Sam Marotta, Buddy Bunn to name a few) have put their vast expertise to work in this growing professional domain.

What are contract underwriters?

They're self-employed and contract with insurers, usually for a defined interval, to underwrite their business. They usually work from home and are usually compensated on a "per case" basis.

With the current shortage of experienced underwriters, many retired underwriters continue to work part-time in this manner.

What are outsourced underwriters?

They differ from underwriters who contract individually directly with insurers. They work for industry firms which offer fee-based underwriting services to insurers.

The number of outsourced underwriting providers has been steadily increasing as insurers find it difficult to hire veteran underwriters and

---

Types of Underwriters

Employer
Home office
Brokerage agency
Contract (self-employed)
Outsource (working for a service provider)

Product Line
Life
Disability Income (DI)
Critical Illness (CI)
Long Term Care (LTC)
Health

Venue
Home office
Regional office
Remote (telecommuting)
Brokerage agency
Service provider

Authority
Chief underwriting officer
Underwriting consultant
Senior underwriter
Junior underwriter
Underwriting trainee

also often require temporary additional underwriting capacity due to high-volume periods.

What is a remote/telecommuting underwriter?

The terms "remote" and "telecommuting" are usually used interchangeably.

However, some prefer to say that "remote" underwriters live beyond commuting distance, whereas "telecommuting" underwriters do not (and thus, can work at home or in the office).

This said, a remote or telecommuting underwriter works soley or mainly from home and is electronically linked to the home office.

He or she may reside in the same city as the home office, working primarily from home most days and also in the office from time to time. On the other hand, a telecommuting underwriter may live on the other side of the country and only rarely visit the home office for meetings.

Is telecommuting/remote underwriting becoming more common?

Very much so, for a number of reasons:

- Insurers report anywhere from 10% to 25% greater productivity from telecommuting underwriters, as compared to those working in the home office.
- Insurers also enjoy lower long-term operating costs on this basis.
- Many underwriters prefer working from home. These days, some underwriters are leaving companies which do not allow telecommuting to take jobs where this opportunity exists.
- For companies having difficulty hiring experienced underwriters in their community, telecommuting becomes a viable way of adding veterans to their staff (as opposed to the problems inherent in training brand new underwriters).

Has telecommuting/remote underwriting interfered with high quality service to producers?

No.

Telecommuting underwriters are expected to maintain appropriate hours and to be as responsive to the field as those in the home office. To preserve their coveted telecommuting status, they know it's imperative to achieve if not exceed employer expectations.

In the future, how do experts see underwriters positioned in relation to insurers?

"Underwriters will increasingly be viewed as free-lance, self-employed professionals who negotiate contract terms for their services with insurers and outsourcing vendors – whether they work on-site at a corporate headquarters or perform their services via telecommuting technologies."

John J. Krinik
Co-author, Getting It Issued (1st and 2nd editions)
On The Risk
Volume 23, Issue 2; April/June 2007

Do all underwriters have essentially the same level of underwriting authority?

No.

The primary measure is the underwriter's "signature limit," which is the amount of insurance coverage he can approve on his own.

One's actual signature limit may be determined by some or all of four factors:

1. Status, with chief underwriters having the highest limit and authority levels grading down from underwriting consultant to

senior underwriter, and being lowest at the junior underwriter level.

2. Experience.

3. Average policy size of the company's business plus the range of face amounts the company typically sees.

4. Company's binding limit with their reinsurer.

In some companies, signature limits are "stacked" so that two underwriters each having a $5,000,000 signature limit can combine their authority to sign $10,000,000.

Is underwriting a science or an art?

It's both.

The "science" comes in the analysis of all the objective evidence at hand.

The "art" derives from being able to see all factors bearing on the risk – the forest and the trees – in a broad context.

It's because of this essential "art" aspect that I can't resist laughing out loud when self-styled "experts" say underwriters can be replaced by machines!

Do underwriters make diagnoses?

No. Diagnosis isn't what we do – although there are times when we probably could from the facts we manage to gather!

We assess individual risks to decide where they fit in broad groupings of risks consisting of many thousands of lives. Then it is the total mortality or morbidity experience of the whole grouping which determines whether this "block of business" is profitable.

How is an underwriter's performance evaluated?

In two ways:

- Objectively, based on quantity and turnaround of cases underwritten, sound decision-making and attention to the needs of producers.
- Subjectively, based on perceptions of management, feedback from others, etc.

How much of an underwriter's performance assessment is based on quantitative factors?

Many companies now use so-called "metrics" to measure productivity, comparing one underwriter to another in terms of established "productivity standards." In my study groups, chief underwriters report that these statistics count for anywhere from 5% to 25% of the underwriter's total performance assessment.

There are some companies which – in my view, anyway – take this metrics concept to the extreme, doing things like meticulously timing each step involved in the underwriter's workday.

One can imagine how an underwriting professional might take exception to this approach, considering that this same invasive process is unlikely to be used with medical officers or actuaries. This is rankling, frankly, because underwriting is every bit as much of a profession as insurance medicine or actuarial science.

One would hope that the primary factor in assessing underwriter performance would be on quality rather than quantity, considering that it is the quality which ultimately goes directly to the insurer's bottom line!

How is the quality of an underwriter's performance evaluated?

With periodic case audits, undertaken primarily (for now, anyway) by veteran underwriters and chief underwriters. The concept of the "designated auditor," however, is gaining traction.

What is a "designated auditor"?

Recently, progressive companies have been designating one or more underwriters to specialize in doing underwriter audits. In some cases, these individuals have responsibility for training as well.

The designated auditor concept promotes consistency in auditing methods and standards, which brings a breath of fresh air for those previously audited by randomly chosen veteran colleagues!

Are all underwriting audits done as part of underwriter performance reviews?

No, there a number of other prevalent reasons why case audits are done:

- To determine if the company's underwriting philosophy and practices are being uniformly applied by underwriters on a case-by-case basis.
- To gather insights as part of an effort to fine-tune underwriting practices.
- To ensure that underwriting is fully compliant with state and federal laws.
- To gauge the areas where additional training is needed.
- When there is reason for concern that an underwriter is not doing his job properly.

Reinsurers do periodic audits of clients' underwriters to ensure that risks passed along (ceded) to the reinsurer are underwritten in a manner consistent with the agreement (treaty) between the insurer and direct writer.

Some proactive insurers are now retaining outside independent underwriting auditors. I do a few of these every year and I have peers who specialize in them.

The big advantage in using outside, independent auditors is getting a "second opinion" on the quality of the technical underwriting being done. This can (and should) extend to evaluating work done by service providers as well.

As a producer, do I care if a company has a sound underwriter audit program?

> *"Anyone who says there isn't time to audit underwriters and apply corrective action bears responsibility for mortality land mines that might be ticking beneath the surface."*

> Daniel M. Farrimon
> Lincoln Re
> *Reinsurance Reporter*
> 3rd Quarter, 1999

In other words, yes!

If a company's underwriters are doing a poor job of making the best possible underwriting decision on every case, you and your client are going to bear the brunt of this, sooner or later.

Any insurer that doesn't devote enough effort to auditing will have adverse downstream consequences, like higher reinsurance rates and unfavorable mortality results.

Can a producer impact an underwriter's performance assessment?

Yes. You are the driver of the company's revenue stream and this gives you serious clout in this context.

Next time an underwriter goes to bat for you on a case, take time to acknowledge his effort in a way that ensures his recognition by his bosses.

Pound for pound, there is NOTHING better you can do to enhance your relationship with an underwriter than giving well-earned positive feedback that gets him well-deserved recognition up the corporate "food chain."

What is the leading method of life insurance distribution?

By the end of 2006, over half of all life business was being placed through brokerage general agencies (BGAs).

Do we need BGAs?

As Gary Dworkin (an old friend and leading BGA) observed in an October 30, 2006 interview article, the market has gotten so complex now that brokers doing business with multiple carriers would be at a huge disadvantage trying to do the best job for their client on their own.

How a large and/or complicated case is prepped for submission to insurers plays a critical role in getting the best possible decision in the shortest possible time. In order to do this on their own, producers would have to divert a huge amount of their time from production.

And even if they could somehow find time, there isn't any way producers themselves can bring to bear expertise equivalent to what the best BGAs provide.

Does the BGA community do its job?

There will always be a few "bad apples" taking liberties with a bottle of "white out." This said, I've never heard anything but "thumbs up" for how the overall brokerage community goes about its business.

What underwriting-related criteria do BGAs consider in choosing which insurers to do business with?

- Quality of service and support
- Retention
- Ability to find capacity to cover jumbo cases

- Competitive underwriting
- Consistent underwriting
- Credible quotes on trial applications

Why should maintaining a consistently superior level of support for producers be a high priority for insurers?

> *"For most, if not all, policyholders in today's electronic world, the face of their insurance company is the agent and the agent's staff, not the home office."*

> Steve Callahan
> Robert E. Nolan Company Management Consultants
> LOMA *Resource* magazine
> March 2008

And you can add to this insightful observation the fact that lack of adequate service and support is the #2 reason – after deficient product offerings – that producers change carriers.

How good is the service and support insurers provide to individual producers and BGAs?

There is no way to characterize this broadly because it varies so widely from insurer to insurer.

Some do a bang-up job; others need to put more effort into meaningful improvements.

What are the 5 main factors that directly contribute to subpar field service?

- "Bean counters" who don't fully understand our business or who take the concept of expense control to the point where it yields negative outcomes.
- Sheer volume overload, which inevitably impinges upon quality service.

- Lack of adequate staffing of underwriters and those who support them.
- Flawed perceptions of producer needs, often as a result of talking too much but listening too little.
- An outmoded and inefficient new business system.

Which of these is most often cited by insurers for inconsistent/poor service?

> *"…they are simply swamped with paper. This condition is of course cyclical and insidious."*

> DuWayne Kilbo
> Windsor Insurance Associates, Inc.
> *Broker World*
> November 2006

What can producers do about service and support problems?

- Make their needs known in plain language.
- Provide credible qualitative and quantitative documentation to buttress their concerns.
- Avoid excessive use of anecdotes; fact of life: there will always be some cases that get tanked no matter how hard everyone tries!
- Be flexible enough to make trade-offs so that your most urgent priorities are tended to.
- Never begin any statement with parenthetical drivel which immediately turns us off. Classic example: "In the 33 years I have been in this business…"
- Then, if they still don't do something about the problems, consider dropping them as an outlet for your business.

If I were a producer, what would I expect in terms of service and support?

- Easily accessible, current and accurate case status updates.
- Reasonable direct access to underwriters on all non-status related

matters.

- Callbacks 100% of the time, either when I leave a message because I can't get through or the question cannot be fully answered at first.
- As much explanation of the basis for an adverse underwriting decision as the underwriter is empowered to provide.
- On rated cases, being told upfront if the decision is eligible for reconsideration and, if so, when and based on what interim criteria.
- On postponed/declined cases, knowing if there is any basis for further consideration in the future and, again, if so, when and based on what interim criteria.
- Oversight on cases left in "underwriting purgatory" for extended periods of time for reasons over which I, as producer, have no control (e.g., outstanding physician's records or all requirements in but no timely decision).
- The privilege of appealing adverse decisions to the chief underwriter – with the solemn promise I will not abuse this privilege or appeal directly over the chief underwriter's head (unless he is fully aware that I'm doing it).

What is an insurer's view on the importance of underwriter/producer relationships?

> *"Understanding the producer's expectations and clearly articulating the reasons for an underwriting decision go a long way in communicating a decision or opening the lines of communication."*

> Paul J. Fedi, FSA, MAAA, FALU
> Assistant Vice President, Life Underwriting
> AXA Equitable Life Insurance Company

What innovations have insurers come up with in recent years to improve underwriting-related service and support to producers?

- Underwriter assistants, who work directly with their under-

writers and handle many service and support functions
historically left solely to underwriters.

- Case managers (also called account executives), an enhancement
of the "underwriter assistant" concept with greater
accountabilities and higher levels of authority.
- Dedicated customer service, new business and underwriting
teams housed together within the company and working
exclusively with one or more agencies.
- Designated underwriters handling jumbo cases only, providing
enhanced support on these cases.
- Designated underwriters working with leading producers,
providing a high level of support.
- And, above all, teleunderwriting, as you will soon see!

**If carriers can provide enhanced service and support for jumbo cases
and top producers, why can't they do the same for all?**

No matter how hard chief underwriters struggle – and struggle they
do, I assure you from personal experience – to get resources allocated,
there is a limit. When that limit is reached, it is a fact of life that
status and success do have their rewards.

Should every insurer provide a "field manual" for its producers?

If "underwriting assistance" ranks #2 in terms of perceived producer
needs from marketing organizations (*Insurance Marketing*, September
2007), then one would think you'd want to have a field manual for
your producers providing as much practical information as possible.
Balanced against this is the cost of creating such a manual, which must
also be kept scrupulously current (lest it becomes everyone's nemesis).

What is the current state of underwriting training and education?

Getting slowly better now after a long and – believe me – much-
regretted "dry spell" from the early 1990s onward.

What caused the "dry spell"?

The absurd notion that education was a luxury, which paved the way for deep budget cuts in educational resources and necessary business travel.

How have things improved in recent years?

Most companies that could afford the luxury of training new underwriters have done a decent job all along. Continuing education, on the other hand, was one of the favorite "sacrificial lambs" when some CFOs went about picking off the "low hanging fruit" in underwriting (and other) budgets.

Growing recognition of the huge impact of underwriting on the corporate bottom line has motivated many insurers to begin reinvesting in continuing education for underwriters.

What resources are out there in the way of continuing education for home office and brokerage agency underwriters?

Not nearly as much as there was years ago when reinsurers had the luxury (sufficient staffing and adequate budget allocations) to provide educational services for their clients!

These are the main resources out there for underwriter education:

- In-house lectures and case clinics presented by medical directors, expert underwriters and others – to the extent that staff resources and productivity demands permit.
- Funding underwriter matriculation in the FALU program.
- Webinars, seminars and other educational offerings provided free or at modest cost, mainly by reinsurers.
- Similar programs, also at low cost, available through underwriting associations.
- Industry publications, most notably those of some larger reinsurers plus *On The Risk* quarterly journal, *Underwriter Alert*, *JournalScan* and *Hot Notes*.
- Independent continuing education, such as my company's State

of the Art™ Continuing Education Program, in which over 2,500 underwriters worldwide have enrolled.

What are underwriting study groups?

Informal gatherings of chief underwriters convened periodically to discuss various industry and underwriting issues (and always with scrupulous attention to anti-trust considerations).

My company currently manages three life underwriting study groups on a non-profit basis for the benefit of the underwriting community. Each has between 25 and 35 members and meets annually for an open forum discussion.

CHAPTER 2

———•———•———•———•———

Underwriting Practices

How do insurers set their underwriting practices?

The main contributors to this process are:

- The chief underwriter and his senior managers
- The chief medical director and his colleagues
- The actuaries

Most companies also get major input from their reinsurers, who have a wealth of knowledge. Furthermore, key aspects of underwriting practices are reflected in the agreement – known as a treaty – between the insurer and the reinsurer.

How important is it for insurers to have well-thought out and reasonably competitive practices?

As important if not more so than any consideration bearing on the new business process:

- If they are too aggressive, they put their bottom line in jeopardy.
- If they are too conservative, they risk losing their best producers and the quality business those producers bring to them.

- If they disdain screening practices prevalent among their competitors, they inevitably incur significant antiselection.
- If they embrace screening practices not deployed by others, they could find themselves on the defensive.

You can see why so much effort goes into the process of setting one's underwriting practices.

What are the factors shaping an insurer's underwriting practices?

- Product portfolio
- Pricing structure
- Underwriting manual guidelines
- Risk-related application/teleinterview questions
- Evidence of insurability requirements
- Preferred risk criteria
- Policies governing appeals, exception-making and "business decisions"
- Retention, automatic reinsurance binding limits and extent of use of facultative reinsurance services

What two main elements of pricing structure impact underwriting practice-setting?

- Pricing assumptions for preferred, standard and substandard classes
- Number of preferred and substandard classes

What do we mean by "underwriting manual"?

The sum of an insurer's underwriting guidelines covering all elements bearing on insurability, including medical impairments, test results, occupations, aviation and avocation activities, driving record and everything else that enters into the assessment of risk.

Are these "guidelines" really better described as "rules"?

No. Rules are for machines!

Besides, no two cases are ever identical.

Real underwriters use manual guidelines as a baseline, to be modified as judgment dictates consistent with all factors bearing on any given risk.

When a manual's guidelines stipulate a certain number of debits for an impairment, the underwriter will assign those debits…unless factors are present in the case at hand which clearly make that risk better or worse.

For example:

The insured has abnormal electrocardiographic findings on a treadmill test done 6 months ago, as reported on the APS. These ECG changes call for a debit of +100. However, his doctor did a stress echocardiogram 2 months later which turned out to be completely normal.

Depending on the specific treadmill abnormalities, a subsequent and normal stress echocardiogram may no longer justify assigning part or even all of the 100 debits.

Conversely, irregularities on the stress echocardiogram may increase the risk implications associated with the treadmill findings, forcing the underwriter to add further debits, based on the nature and extent of those further findings.

In many cases, there are no factors present of this kind and the debit cited in the manual guidelines is used. Where there are such factors to consider, however, it is the responsibility of the underwriter to endeavor to make the best decision possible after careful review of all information at hand.

Do most insurers create their own underwriting manual internally?

No.

Based on a 2007 survey of over 120 U.S. life companies, less than 10% have their own in-house underwriting manual. Thus, the vast majority use one or more reinsurance manuals.

Why do so few companies have in-house manuals?

The research, analysis, writing and maintaining of an internal underwriting manual is both a costly and formidable undertaking. Total cost can easily run to the mid-to-high six figures.

Furthermore, there are obstacles conferred by lean staffing, high productivity demands and the fact that the best candidates to create the manual are usually the most knowledgeable persons on the firing line handling tough cases.

Do most insurers use only one reinsurance manual?

Over 40% who rely on reinsurance manuals use just one. The remainder use two or even more.

Do those who use two or more consider one to be their primary manual?

Yes, typically with the agreement of all of the reinsurers with whom they have treaties. The others are used for additional perspective, as needed.

Do insurers using reinsurer manuals modify the guidelines in those manuals to suit their own company practices?

Yes, but for the most part only covering a relatively small number of topics.

They do this because business they fully retain is unaffected by reinsurance treaty arrangements and, even on business which is ceded to reinsurers, direct companies typically have latitude in this regard.

How faithfully are underwriting manuals kept current to reflect the latest developments and new knowledge which could influence their guidelines?

In our competitive environment there is plenty of incentive to continually update and fine-tune one's practices!

Nevertheless, the extent of manual maintenance varies widely. The driver here is how much the company is willing to divert its most talented staff from production to get this job done. Given the status of production, you can guess what the answer often is.

How does an insurer develop its insurance application?

Typically it is a multidisciplinary undertaking, led by the chief underwriting officer with help from the actuaries, medical directors and chief claims officer, along with focal input from the law, compliance and POS departments.

How many applications will an insurer have?

At least one for each product line (life, DI, CI, LTC and health) and usually several in each line depending on the nature of the products. They may also have one or more simplified issue applications which contain far fewer risk-related questions.

Do the insurer's application forms have to be approved?

Yes, by the insurance department in every state where the insurer writes new business. The commissioner and his colleagues may mandate that changes be made before the application is approved.

What are the three main components of the application?

We typically designate them as Parts I, II and III:

Part I – Essential details covering the plan of insurance, amount applied for, the proposed insured's name, address, date of birth and so on. The "lay" (non-medical) risk-related questions are also included in the Part I, covering such things as aviation, avocation, occupation, driving record, etc.

Part II – Medical history and related questions.

Part III – Completed by the producer and sometimes called the "agent's certificate." Unlike the Parts I and II, the Part III is not signed by the proposed insured.

How is the application taken?

Historically – and in more than a few companies, currently – it was a paper document completed by the producer, based on asking the proposed insured the questions in order and then recording the answers.

Today, it is more apt to be completed and even signed electronically. Some insurers put their applications at their website, especially on business applied for directly by the proposed insured in the absence of a producer.

The greatest underwriting innovation of the modern era, teleunderwriting, is fast becoming the dominant mode for completing the risk-related application questions. With teleunderwriting, these questions are asked and the answers are recorded during a telephone interview with the proposed insured, undertaken by a trained interviewer.

We will cover teleunderwriting in considerable depth later on because every producer needs a clear understanding of what teleunderwriting is and how it works.

How is an application signed in the teleunderwriting setting?

In one of three ways:

- On policy delivery, with wet signature
- Electronically
- By voice signature

What if the application is incomplete?

The file goes into AVOIDABLE "suspended animation" while the missing information is recorded and forwarded on to the home office!

One of the huge advantages conferred by both Internet-based and teleinterview application-taking is that there are no "incompletes."

Why?

Because the application cannot be forwarded on until every question is answered.

CHAPTER 3

The Concept of Requirements

What do we mean by "requirements"?

Information which must be obtained and reviewed by the underwriter before underwriting can be completed and a decision made on insurability.

What are the two main kinds of requirements?

- Mandatory; also known both as screening and "age and amount" requirements
- Elective

What is meant by "age and amount"?

Whether or not a requirement is mandated depends on the age of the proposed insured and the amount of insurance applied for.

Who determines if an "elective" requirement is ordered?

It depends on the requirement.

Some elective requirements are triggered by findings on screening requirements. This pertains mainly to laboratory tests, where the additional requirements are known as "reflexive" tests.

In all other cases, elective requirements are ordered by the underwriter based on his judgment as to what he needs in order to adequately assess the risk.

What are the main considerations bearing on the decision whether or not to make use of an underwriting requirement?

Based on a recent survey, these were the top-ranked factors:

1. Claims experience
2. Impact on reinsurance pricing
3. Reinsurer recommendations
4. Input from actuaries
5. Input from medical directors
6. Impact on "application-to-issue" turnaround time
7. Relative cost, as compared to other options
8. Findings on protective value studies
9. Competitor practices

What are "protective value studies"?

In-depth studies undertaken by chief underwriters, actuaries and, where appropriate, medical officers to determine the extent to which a given requirement produces tangible value. "Value" is defined as the amount of worthwhile information bearing on insurability which the requirement provides.

Companies do these studies internally to determine if it is cost-effective to use a given requirement. They also rely on the comparative handful of published studies in this regard.

Is a "cost/benefit study" synonymous with a protective value study?

The implication in "cost/benefit" is that the return on investment

(ROI) drives the assessment. However, protective value studies typically consider the cost of a requirement as well. Therefore, for practical purposes, I use the terms interchangeably.

Call them what you will, they both focus on this question: Is the anticipated return from a requirement significantly greater than the cost of using it, and, if so, how does the magnitude of the expected return compare to that of other potential requirements which might be used instead?

CHAPTER 4

———•———•———•———•———

Screening Requirements

What are the primary screening requirements widely used by life insurers?

Primary Screening Requirements in Life Underwriting

- MIB codes
- Attending physician's statement (APS)
- Non-medical
- Paramedical
- Medical examination
- Teleinterview (to be covered in a separate chapter)
- Blood profile
- Urine profile
- Oral fluid profile
- Prostate specific antigen (PSA) test
- Electrocardiogram (ECG)
- Treadmill stress test (exercise ECG)
- Chest x-ray
- Pharmacy (Rx) profile
- Motor vehicle report (MVR)
- Inspection report

Are there additional tests which at least some insurers now use in screening?

Yes, but because the majority – at least for now – do not screen with them, we will cover them under REFLEXIVE REQUIREMENTS.

Attending Physicians Statement (APS)

How important is the APS in underwriting?

"...we continue to believe the APS remains the most valuable underwriting tool in terms of underwriting protective value."

Nancy Caron and Bill Moore
Swiss Re
On The Risk
Volume 21, Issue 3
September 2005

Nancy and Bill pretty much summed it up.

Without access to medical records, a substantial share of applications, including nearly all for substantial amounts of coverage and/or with significant medical histories, simply could not be underwritten.

Are medical records ordered on an age/amount or on an elective basis?

Both.

At some face amounts applied for, most (but not all) insurers will require medical records at most or all ages.

This threshold amount at which routine reports are pursued has a J-shaped appearance when illustrated graphically because it is typically lower in children, adolescents and older ages as compared to young adults.

In the case of children and adolescents, large sums of insurance are rarely appropriate without extenuating financial considerations, so we are concerned about medical antiselection.

As one ages beyond young adulthood, the incidence of chronic disease increases, gradually at first and then more steeply at age 65+.

Under what circumstances do underwriters order medical records electively?

Mainly when there is an admitted (or suspected) medical history that could impact insurability.

On what percentage of its life applications would the average insurer be likely to require an APS?

This is virtually impossible to determine in a meaningful manner because the answer for any one company is impacted by so many factors.

The most important factor here, as you might imagine, is the carrier's primary market. If they do a sizeable amount of older age business, the APS becomes the rule, not the exception, compared to where most of the policies are written on young and middle-aged adults.

Roughly one carrier in every 10 will get an APS on < 10% of new apps, whereas a larger percentage will order an APS on anywhere from 30-60%. In the most recent survey we have seen, the most prevalent range of elective APS ordering was between 20% and 24% of new life applications.

What are the three main sources from which we get medical records?

- Doctors
- Clinics

- Hospitals

What is the cost of an APS?

It ranges widely but we wouldn't be surprised if the average out-of-pocket cost is at least $55-75 in 2009…and steadily rising. Indeed, we are told a recent survey showed that the average was $65.

In addition to out-of-pocket expenditures, are there any other significant costs associated with the APS?

Yes.

First, the majority of carriers use service providers to obtain medical records and there is a fee connected with this service.

There is also a major indirect cost.

An APS, on average, takes far longer to review than any other requirement in our armamentarium and, as a result, a significant portion of the underwriter's day may be consumed by reading and extracting salient information from medical records.

What factors influence the indirect cost of the APS?

- Some are quiet literally HUGE. Military records are the worst "offenders" in this regard.
- Most consist of photocopies of records, which means there is a lot of information with little if any bearing on underwriting which nevertheless must be reviewed lest any critical nugget of information be overlooked.
- Sometimes the papers are not in chronological order.
- Not uncommonly, something of significance will be encountered halfway through a 50 page report, forcing the underwriter to go back over previous pages and reconsider content which previously may have appeared insignificant.
- Medical records are replete with medical acronyms and other

forms of "medical shorthand," some of which can be fairly
esoteric and compel the underwriter to check out their meaning.

- And if all of this weren't enough to induce a tension headache,
physician handwriting is infamous for its illegibility!

Do insurers ever outsource the review of the APS?

This service has been available for years. Last year, I did an informal
survey of companies represented in my study groups and found that
most had never done this and some that had experimented with APS
summarizing soon discontinued the practice due to unsatisfactory
results.

On the other hand, a few carriers were pleased with what they got
on outsourced APS summaries and it wouldn't surprise me if further
headway is made in this domain in the years ahead.

How long does it take to get the average APS?

When using an APS gathering service, some insurers now report
that they consistently get most medical records in 12 to 15 working
days. While this is a big improvement over what was true in the
past, the APS still remains by far the slowest requirement, overall, in
underwriting.

Are there any other important issues related to the APS?

Yes. The insidious decline in the quantity and quality of information
on "sensitive" impairments.

What are these "sensitive" impairments?

- Psychiatric disorders
- Alcohol and drug abuse
- Sexual, emotional and other forms of abuse endured by the
applicant
- Impairments in sexual function (which can have important

underlying medical causes)
- Sexually transmitted diseases
- Genetically mediated diseases
- Results of genetic tests

How do we compensate for the dearth of essential information related to sensitive impairments?

With teleinterviews, where applicants have the opportunity to be more disclosing as compared to what their physicians feel comfortable sharing with us.

Have these issues with medical records caused insurers to explore alternatives?

Absolutely, considering how medical records directly impact the two main elements of senior management's agenda where underwriting is concerned: lowered business acquisition costs and reduced 32--to-issue turnaround time.

What is the main alternative in this regard?

Teleinterviews, as you will soon see.

Non-Medical

What are the five alternative ways in which insurers can gather medical history information from proposed insureds?

- Non-medicals
- Paramedicals
- Medical exams
- Internet-based interviews
- Teleinterviews

What do we mean by a "non-medical"?

This is the term used when the producer takes the proposed insured's medical history as part of completing the application.

What are the strengths of the non-medical?

- Fast
- No out-of-pocket cost to insurer

What are its disadvantages?

When you think about it, it is inherently illogical to ask the person whose income depends on the outcome to act as the intermediary in gathering the information most apt to affect that outcome.

Then, too, most underwriters would agree that non-medicals provide the least information of the five alternatives – not to mention the highest prevalence of butchered spelling of medical terms and drug names!

Where do insurers make the greatest use of non-medicals?

On children, adolescents and young adults, where the incidence of medical impairments is far lower than at older ages.

What is the future of the non-medical?

It will eventually disappear in favor of teleinterviews.

Does this mean that producers will no longer need to inquire about their clients' medical history?

Not at all.

How can you hope to counsel a client on what to apply for if you don't have a satisfactory understanding of his prospects for insurability?

The fine art of the FACT-FINDING INTERVIEW is intrinsic to being a successful producer and must be universally embraced.

If I were a producer, I would use the non-medical form informally as my guide when trying to get a sufficient picture of my client's health status.

PARAMEDICAL

What is a paramedical?

An aggregation of four main tasks, primarily completed by persons who have, in most cases, been trained as medical technologists.

What are these four tasks?

- Verifying the identity of the individual
- Performing a small number of physical measurements
- Taking the medical history
- Collecting one or more bodily fluids for laboratory analysis

Do some of these tasks confer more value for insurers than others?

They all bring significant value...however, with the advent of teleinterviews, some companies have now discontinued having the medical history taken during paramedicals.

Why not take the medical history twice and potentially increase the amount of useful information?

This is not a good idea for three reasons:

- I doubt there would be much if any additional value. From

all I have seen, teleinterview medical histories are far superior overall and it is unlikely that significant additional information would be found in the medical history taken by the paramedical technician.

- It increases the cost of the paramedical.
- It is unlikely clients will take too well to being asked about their medical history twice when applying just once! Redundancy is one thing insurers must strive to eliminate.

How are most paramedicals done?

On a mobile basis, where the paramedical technician goes to the place of residence or employment of the proposed insured.

Do insurers usually approve more than one paramedical service provider to do paramedicals on their business?

Yes.

The average number of approved providers probably averages between three and four. Only a handful of companies use just one provider or, conversely, appoint all who offer this service.

Do all paramedical technicians do their work exclusively for one provider firm?

No. This is far less common now than it once was.

When did the paramedical become a widely used requirement?

In the mid-to-late 1970s. Then, in the 1980s, volumes increased exponentially with the advent of widespread blood and urine testing.

Why did paramedicals become so appealing to insurers?

Because they are much less costly and usually completed sooner than examinations by physicians.

Who schedules the majority of paramedicals?

Producers and their staffs. However, the trend toward having them scheduled electronically via services provided by industry vendors is increasing.

Is there value in a producer preparing his client for a paramedical?

ABSOLUTELY! Fact is, the failure to do so is a huge mistake with potentially major consequences as regards insurability.

This is so important that we will devote an entire chapter to it further on.

Do most insurers audit their paramedical providers?

They probably all do in one context: to make sure they are not over-charged or inadvertently billed for work done for other carriers.

Some ask their underwriters to provide feedback if they notice something that's not quite right on a given paramedical, but this is far too sporadic to do much good.

Unfortunately, the type of in-depth audit I believe insurers should being doing on paramedical (and all other service) providers isn't undertaken by more than a handful of insurers.

What are the most prevalent issues insurers have with paramedical providers?

- Absence of sufficient details on medical histories.
- Measurements not fully recorded, especially additional blood pressure readings when stipulated or clearly needed.
- Signatures missing.
- Problems with ECG quality (parameds facilitate most screening ECGs).
- Paucity of comments by examiners with regard to such things as

tattooing.

From my perspective there is one more issue: the fact that there are things which could be – but mostly aren't – done to enhance the value of the paramedical. These include:

- Waist circumference – ideally, both waist and hip circumference – measurement. This should be routine because it has huge value in the assessment of weight-related concerns.
- Pulse pressure, calculated from blood pressure readings.
- Consistent reporting of the presence of tattoos.
- The ratio of arm-to-ankle blood pressure would have tremendous underwriting value on all applicants ages 65 and over as well as on middle-aged and old diabetics and longtime heavy smokers. Whether this can be credibly done by paramedical technicians has yet to be determined.

Will most insurers share paramedicals done for them with another insurer to whom the proposed insured currently or subsequently applies?

A recent survey tells us that the majority will do so if they receive a signed, dated and still valid authorization. Some of them, however, would ask that the other carrier(s) share the cost since they are also sharing in the value.

Medical Examination

How does a paramedical differ from a medical examination?

- Medicals are done by physicians, not technicians.
- Paramedicals are limited to a handful of physical measurements; medical exams are (in theory at least) just what their name suggests: a comprehensive physical examination of the proposed insured.

- On average, it takes longer to get a medical exam done.
- Medical exams cost significantly more than paramedicals.

Do most insurers make at least some use of medical examinations for screening purposes?

Yes, the vast majority still require them, albeit on a declining number of cases.

Do most insurers permit an exam to be done by the proposed insured's personal physician?

A 2003 survey in *On The Risk* revealed that over half never allow this and a few others do so only on an occasional basis in the face of extraordinary circumstances.

In my view, this is totally inappropriate and should never be countenanced. The risk of nondisclosure far outweighs any possible advantages.

Does evidence show that medical exams have enough marginal added value over paramedicals to justify their use?

If there is any published evidence for this, I have not seen it.

The above-mentioned survey revealed that insurers find more errors on MD exams than on paramedicals.

One unpublished study done years ago got my attention because it showed that medical examiners were not looking at the eyes of proposed insureds. By this I mean checking for pathological abnormalities associated and commonly encountered in diabetes and high blood pressure.

This logically raises the question: If they don't do this routine step during insurance exams, what else aren't they doing?

Will medical examinations no longer be used in the future?

Probably not entirely, especially where jumbo amounts of coverage at older ages are concerned.

However, their use has declined consistently in recent years. This is probably due mainly to the cost differential between exams and paramedicals more than to any other factor, based on a survey where 8 out of 10 insurers felt the cost difference was not justifiable.

Blood Profile

What is a blood profile?

A panel of blood tests used routinely in both insurance and clinical screening.

What are the typical components of a screening blood profile?

See the table **Typical Components in Insurance Screening Blood Profiles** on the following page.

Is all of this done on a single blood specimen?

Yes, and reflexive blood tests (see below) can also be performed on that same specimen for a defined interval of time (usually 30 days, measured from the date the specimen arrives at the laboratory).

Is a blood profile expensive?

Actually, it is remarkably inexpensive, especially when you compare the costs to insurers to the prices I have seen in clinical medicine. Low cost is one reason blood profiles have become one of the most widely used underwriting tools in North America.

Typical Components in Insurance Screening Blood Profiles

Diabetes
- Glucose (blood sugar)
- Fructosamine

Lipids
- Total cholesterol (TC)
- High-density lipoprotein cholesterol (HDL-C)
- Low-density lipoprotein cholesterol (LDL-C)
- Triglycerides
- TC-to-HDL-C ratio (calculated from its components)

Kidney
- BUN (blood urea nitrogen)
- Creatinine
- Uric acid – some labs do this test; others don't – I wish they all did
- Glomerular filtration rate (eGFR) – a calculation, reported routinely by some labs but available from all if the insurer wishes

Liver
- Aspartate aminotransferase (AST, SGOT)
- Alanine aminotransferase (ALT, SGPT)
- Gamma-glutamyltransferase (GGT, GGTP)
- Alkaline phosphatase (AP)
- Total bilirubin

Serum Proteins
- Total protein
- Albumin
- Globulin

HIV-1 test

At what face amount threshold do most life insurers require a blood profile?

The most prevalent threshold at all ages from 18 to 75+ is $100,000.

Most companies that use a lower threshold will do so at ages 55 or over. By age 65, roughly 40% now require a blood profile in the range of $50,000 and I wouldn't be surprised to see this percentage grow in the near future.

Why?

Most of the value from blood profiles emerges after age 40 and it escalates steeply at age 55+. The more value an insurer gets, the more tests it will do.

Would it be unwise for an insurer to set a significantly higher threshold for blood profile screening than its competitors?

Absolutely, because this would invite antiselection. Individuals who know they have abnormalities on these tests would be disposed to seek coverage from companies that do not require the test.

In today's market, this is a pretty big risk to take.

What do the results of these tests tell us?

See the **Blood Profile Test and Implications** table on the following page. We're going to cover the diabetes, lipid and liver tests later in this book.

Blood Profile Test	Implications
HIV-1 test	Positive test means infection with the HIV-1 virus, which causes AIDS. A confirmatory test is always done on a positive screening test.
BUN	Significant elevations are usually due to a kidney impairment. Minimal elevations are not important as an isolated finding. Below-normal BUN occurs in advanced liver disease.
Creatinine	Elevations are mainly due to kidney damage. Creatinine is far superior to BUN because even minimal elevations are significant at older ages. When it is due to kidney damage, it does not become elevated until $\geq 50\%$ of kidney function is lost.
Glomerular Filtration Rate	Reported as eGFR. Low levels (mainly < 60) equate to kidney damage.
Uric Acid	Elevations associated with increased risk of gout and circulatory disease.
Total Protein	Significance depends on levels of globulin and albumin.
Albumin	This is blood albumin; not to be confused with urine albumin. Elevations are not significant; low levels are strongly associated with chronic disease as well as with physical frailty in the elderly.
Globulin	Elevations as well as below normal readings are usually due to disease and are always significant to insurability.

URINE PROFILE

What is a urine profile?

A combination of test components performed on a urine specimen.

What are the usual components of an insurance screening urine profile?

Typical Components of Insurance Screening Urine Profiles	
• Specific gravity	• Marker for presence of red blood cells
• Urine creatinine	• Marker for presence of white blood cells
• Urine glucose	• Cotinine test
• Urine protein	• Cocaine test

Is a urine profile expensive?

Like the blood profile, it is incredibly inexpensive.

At what face amount threshold do most life insurers require a urine profile?

Most companies require a urine profile every time they require a blood profile. Some do urine profiles at smaller face amounts than blood testing because the percentage of positive cotinine and cocaine tests is much higher at face amounts under $100,000.

What do the results of these urine profile components tell us?

We will defer cotinine and cocaine until later because these are topics with major implications for underwriters, producers and clients.

See the **Urine Profile Test and Implications** table on the following page for a brief look at the rest of the components usually included on insurance urine screening profiles.

Urine Profile Test	Implications
Specific Gravity	Measures urine density and helps to put other test results in perspective.
Urine Creatinine	It is not like blood creatinine and is used mainly in context with the urine protein and albumin tests.
Urine Glucose	Used to detect undiagnosed or inadequately treated diabetes. May be positive due to recent food intake or other insignificant causes.
Urine Protein	Marker for possible kidney damage; mainly used in conjunction with microalbumin test. (This will be discussed further on.)
Red Blood Cells	Urine is screened for traces of blood; if positive, the number of cells is reported. When red blood cells are present, our concern is for kidney damage at all ages as well as cancer of the kidney, bladder or urinary tract at older ages.
White Blood Cells	Urine is screened for traces of these cells. If they are present, the number of cells is reported. White blood cells are seldom as significant as red blood cells and are mainly due to minor urinary tract infections.

Is HIV-1 testing done on urine?

Not often because it is mainly done on blood and oral fluid tests.

ORAL FLUID TESTING

Is this the same thing as "saliva" testing?

No.

Unfortunately, many people use the term "saliva" as if it were synonymous with oral fluid. In fact, some people still call it the "spit test"!

Testing saliva would not be worthwhile; thus, what is tested for here is not saliva.

What is tested for?

A very specific fluid called mucosal transudate.

How is oral fluid testing done?

A stick with a pad on it is placed in between the cheek and gum. This pad absorbs mucosal transudate fluid. When it has been held in place for the designated amount of time, it is removed, placed in a tube for mailing and sent to the lab for analysis.

What components are on the oral fluid test?

- Cotinine
- Cocaine
- HIV-1

Are there any other components which could be added?

A great deal of research is being done in clinical medicine with an eye toward expanding the use of oral fluid as a screening test.

For our purposes, one would think methamphetamine testing would be feasible. The main issue, as I understand it, is the amount of fluid collected may not be sufficient to run additional tests on just the one specimen.

How many companies currently use oral fluid testing on at least some of their business?

In the last survey, 37% were using it.

Why do many companies opt to use oral fluid?

> *"Oral fluid testing continues to provide real value in a noninvasive manner even for small amounts of applied-for insurance. For larger amounts up to $250,000 and more – savings is enhanced even further with returns on testing investment exceeding 40% per year for ages over 40."*

> Rick Bergstrom, FSA, MAAA
> Consulting Actuary
> Seattle
> *On The Risk*
> 21, 1(2005):63

At what ages and face amounts is oral fluid mainly used?

Younger ages (45 and under) and smaller face amounts.

The number of companies using it at ages 45 and under is twice as high as at older ages. The face amount range where it is mainly used is $100,000 and under, although some companies go as high as $500,000.

Why isn't oral fluid used more widely for insurance screening?

Two things hold it back from wider use:

- Resistance by some producers to collecting the specimens (which, when you think about it, doesn't make much sense).
- The fact that blood and urine are done at comparatively low face

amounts. If you require a paramedical, it just makes sense to collect blood or urine instead, because they have more components with underwriting value.

I, for one, see considerable merit in using oral fluid at lower face amount thresholds than it is currently done by most user companies.

Why?

Because the % of applicants who test positive for cotinine, cocaine and HIV-1 is inverse to face amount.

In other words, you get far more positive tests for all three components when you test at $50,000 rather than $100,000, and more still at $25,000.

Are oral fluid specimens collected by paramedical technicians?

They can be and some companies insist on this. But they can be collected by anyone capable of following a couple of simple instructions.

Right now, 2 out of every 3 companies using oral fluid ask their producers to collect the oral fluid specimens, and nearly half of the rest of them allow for producer collection as an alternative to paramedical collection.

Why ask producers to collect oral fluid?

Two reasons: cost and turnaround time.

You see your client face-to-face and oral fluid is so easy to collect. If you collect it, the company saves the cost of having it collected by the paramed technician.

And you benefit as well because the sample is tested sooner and thus most cases where it is required will be approved that much faster.

As we said, oral fluid is used mainly at younger ages and smaller amounts, the vast majority of which are approved as applied for without getting an APS.

So why do some companies allow agents to have paramed people collect them or even, in 1 out of 5 companies surveyed, insist it be a paramedical collector?

Best as I can tell, some carriers are just less disposed to ask you to do it than others. Then, too, some companies have a lot of independent producers from whom they get comparatively little business and so they worry about the tests being done wrong (which can mean doing it again, or worse, closing the file).

Prostate Specific Antigen (PSA)

What is PSA?

A tumor marker test used to screen for prostate cancer. PSA is the only tumor marker currently used to screen for cancer in people who are not necessarily considered to be at increased risk for the malignancy in question.

How is it done?

It is a blood test and can be tested for in a routine screening blood sample.

Do most insurers routinely screen male applicants with PSA?

Roughly 2 out of 3 companies do it at some age and amount threshold.

At what age do these companies typically begin requiring a PSA test?

Typically around age 55 or so.

What testing threshold is most prevalent?

In the $100,000 to $200,000 range; a small number start higher or lower.

What is considered a normal result on PSA testing?

All men will have some measurable amount of PSA unless they have had their prostate gland removed and do not have metastatic prostate cancer.

There is some debate among experts as to what to use as the lower limit of normal. Some say 4.0 nanograms while others argue that because of the increased incidence of prostate cancer at lower levels, the threshold for an abnormal PSA test should be 2.5 nanograms.

What do insurers do when PSA is elevated on an insurance screening test?

Practices vary widely depending upon a variety of factors, including the applicant's age, his medical and family histories and the level of PSA elevation.

There are several scenarios where postponement pending further evaluation by the insured's urologist or primary care physician is fairly common:

- The insured is known to be at high risk, mainly due to family history.
- The insured is relatively young, such as 55 or younger.
- The reading is > 10; perhaps lower depending upon other factors present and the company's underwriting philosophy.

Could an argument be made to postpone all cases where PSA is elevated?

Yes – simply because of the fact that undiagnosed prostate cancer has a higher probability of being present and we cannot know if this cancer is aggressive until it has been studied by a pathologist.

Is there any test which can be done in underwriting to further assess someone with an elevated PSA test?

Yes, a test called "free PSA" (fPSA). This test distinguishes between two types of PSA. One is attached to certain proteins and the other is not. The free PSA test tells us what % of each type is present.

How does fPSA help assess an elevated PSA?

If the free portion of PSA is too low, the risk is increased.

This is all rather complicated and there are differing views as to what should be considered "significantly low."

Do most companies that use PSA screening make use of this additional test?

Yes, with widely varying guidelines as to when – based on age, face amount and degree of screening PSA reading – the free PSA test should be done.

What is the underwriting implication of an abnormal free PSA test?

That the case is best postponed because the risk of prostate cancer is too high to accept on any basis.

Have there been occasions where insurance PSA screening has led to the discovery and curative treatment of unsuspected prostate cancer?

Absolutely, just as there would be in a clinical screening test. No doubt more than a few lives have been saved on this basis.

If an applicant is found to have an elevated PSA test, do insurers send

the results to him or to his doctor?

I have never seen a survey of companies regarding this practice. However, I do know many companies are doing this, based on discussions I have had with them at meetings, etc.

To my way of thinking, the possible risks inherent in not disclosing abnormal PSA results – whether or not adverse action is taken – would be too great to overlook.

In my view – and I am very conservative on this point – it is desirable to make certain every proposed insured who has a PSA test gets the results, either directly or via his physician, regardless of what the result is.

This is useful from the applicant's point of view because even a normal test may have patient care significance when taken in context with PSA tests done previously or to be done in the future.

Companies, of course, may have concerns with doing this routinely and the decision to do so or not does rest with the insurer.

Do women ever have a positive PSA test?

While it is extremely rare for a woman to have enough PSA to reach the threshold for elevation, women do manufacture minute amounts of PSA and there are scenarios where that amount has significance regarding their health.

Fortunately, we don't have to worry about this issue in life insurance testing!

Electrocardiogram (ECG)

Why do you use "ECG" instead of "EKG"?

Because ECG is the preferred acronym, if only because there is no "k" in the term.

What is an ECG?

A heart test done using a device called a "string galvanometer," which can record heartbeats graphically.

When the test is done, 12 "leads" (wires) are connected to different places on the person's anatomy and readings are taken at each place. Six leads are on the extremities (called "limb leads") and six are from the center of the chest across to near the left armpit (called "chest leads").

Taken together, the two-dimensional images recorded from these 12 views give us a "picture" of the heartbeat's sequential components, including heart rate and rhythm as well as the presence of potential abnormalities within the heart.

How are these readings recorded?

On a continuous strip of specialized paper, which is then usually cut into segments representing each of the 12 leads and then mounted to save time when interpreting what the tracings (as we call them) mean.

Do paramedical technicians do ECGs for us?

The vast majority of screening ECGs are done paramedically.

Who interprets these ECGs?

Medical directors do a fair share of them, as do nurses and lay underwriters.

Are you saying that lay underwriters can read ECGs?

Sure...at least to the extent needed in an insurance screening context.

There are always a few difficult ones where they need help from nurses or medical directors. This said, the best-trained and most experienced underwriters can do much more ECG assessment than merely screen out the normal ones.

What happens if the ECG is abnormal?

At least 30% of all screening ECGs are, technically, "abnormal." However, the vast majority of these are trivial abnormalities having no significance as far as insurability is concerned.

When an abnormality isn't trivial and cannot be ignored, what factors determine how it impacts underwriting?

- Specific finding.
- Gender.
- Age.
- Whether or not this same finding or one related to it was present on an ECG done previously.
- If it was present on a prior ECG and we have information about more than one prior ECG, whether it is present on all of them or appeared subsequent to an ECG where it was not present.
- Whether it is an isolated finding or other abnormalities are present.
- When other abnormalities are present, whether or not they are related to one another in terms of reflecting possible underlying cardiac pathology.
- The applicant's cardiovascular profile.
- The applicant's medical history.
- The results of any further tests done by the insurer and/or the applicant's doctor in the wake of the discovery of this finding.

Do insurers make extensive use of ECGs in screening?

Not when you compare what we did in the 20th century to what we do today.

At what ages and amounts are ECGs most often required?

The typical threshold age is 45 and the typical face amount range at that age is between $250,000 and $750,000. However, some companies still persist in getting them at high face amounts as young as age 25. In addition, others will insist on them for amounts well under $250,000 in the age 55-65+ range.

Do ECGs provide enough protective value to justify their use at the levels where they are currently required?

I find no compelling evidence suggesting this is true, but obviously many people must believe otherwise or they would be used much less than they are.

What are the arguments against using ECGs?

- They are more costly than blood and urine tests.
- They are conspicuously less convenient for the client.
- They require more handling.
- Their assessment is both objective and subjective. Subjectivity often translates to two people seeing the same finding differently (or only one of the people even believing it is present). This leads to counterproductive discussions with the proposed insured's physician, especially if the case is rated or postponed due to the alleged finding.
- There are much better options available now; there are new tests that can be done on routine blood specimens and confer considerable protective value without all this baggage.

Will ECG screening decrease?

It has to, because it cannot compete with the alternative option. There isn't much reason to use them under age 50 and I would expect their deployment at these younger ages will end first.

Ultimately, the ECG is doomed because of drawbacks incompatible with the "fast, cheaper, better" mandate of senior management.

TREADMILL STRESS TEST

What is a treadmill stress test?

An ECG done during and after exercise, following a specified protocol established by cardiologists (which is why we also call this an "exercise ECG" despite the fact that "treadmill stress test" is a better choice of terms).

What is the advantage of exercise, as compared to doing it when the person is at rest?

Exercise increases the demand for oxygen, which means that if there is any blockage in the arteries that does not show up when the heart needs blood at rest (oxygen is carried in the blood, of course), then with the increased blood flow required for exercise these blockages are more likely to lead to tell-tale abnormalities on the ECG.

Do most insurers currently use treadmill stress tests to screen proposed insureds?

Yes, over 60% in the last survey.

At what ages and amounts are treadmills most likely to be required?

Use increases dramatically at ages 55 and over and few companies do them for under $1,000,000 at this age. In fact, over half of them don't get a treadmill at age 55 until > $2.5 million or even over $5,000,000.

If insurers screen with treadmills, do they require them on the elderly?

Yes, 2 out of 3 using treadmills still require them at age 75.

Do you have any concerns here?

Not to sound like an alarmist, but there is risk associated with these tests. People drop dead during treadmills, albeit very rarely when they are properly done and a cardiologist is present.

My concern is that this is a risk we just don't need to take any longer.

What are the arguments for discontinuing the use of treadmill stress testing as a screening requirement?

- They are far too expensive, costing anywhere from $500 to $1000.
- They are far too slow.
- They are client-unfriendly. What do "financial services" and performing on a treadmill like a caged gerbil have in common?
- They are too subjective. There is an even a higher incidence of disagreement than with resting ECGs because they are more difficult to interpret.
- The risk of a tragedy – death during an insurance treadmill – is not one that insurers should be willing to accept.
- There are cheaper, faster and better alternatives which do not have all of this baggage.

Does this mean you would NEVER order a treadmill test for underwriting purposes?

No – but there is a difference between routine screening and ordering the occasional test "for cause" when it is clearly the best available alternative to postponing or declining a big case.

Will the treadmill stress disappear as an underwriting screening requirement?

For all of the foregoing reasons, it must.

There was a time when one could fashion a case, if only based on protective value in a vacuum, for using treadmills as screening tests.

That time has passed.

If I were a producer, I could not justify putting my client through this experience if I had a choice. And when almost 40% of companies have abandoned screening treadmill testing, I may very well have that choice.

CHEST X-RAY

How many insurers still use screening chest x-rays?

Less than 20%.

When do these companies usually require them?

Some require a chest x-ray at ages as young as 25 for amounts as low as > $1,000,000. The majority set a threshold roughly 5 times higher.

What are the advantages of chest x-rays?

If you can think of one, let me know.

What are the drawbacks?

Essentially all of the adversities associated with treadmill tests plus the fact that they involve exposure to a carcinogen (cancer-causing agent).

What is the absolute risk of radiation exposure from a chest x-ray?

Extremely low, but this doesn't matter because any such exposure is utterly incompatible with financial services.

What do we do if chest x-rays show abnormalities?

Assuming these abnormalities really exist (based on second opinions and further testing) and have risk significance, it depends entirely on the magnitude of their ostensible significance.

Would you consider ordering a chest x-ray "for cause"?

There could be a scenario where this is the only perceived alternative to postponing or declining. This said, I would do everything I could to avoid it.

Will we stop using chest x-rays to screen in the near future?

Twenty years ago, clinical medicine disavowed screening with chest x-rays unless there was a legitimate reason. One would hope we would follow their example.

PHARMACY (Rx) PROFILES

What is a pharmacy (Rx) profile?

A report of all prescriptions filled by the applicant over a specific interval of time.

How do insurers access this information?

It is provided by several industry service firms. They, in turn, get the data from companies called pharmacy benefit managers (PBMs), who, in turn, get it from pharmacies with whom they are connected.

Do clients know this profile is being used?

They should because it is clearly referenced in the authorization they must sign.

Can insurers get profiles on all persons who apply for coverage?

No.

Currently, Rx profile providers get data on about 70-75% of proposed insureds. Some people are outside the loop for various reasons or their data are stored by a PBM that does not participate in this system.

How quickly does the underwriter get this information?

Almost instantaneously as it comes electronically once a request is made.

How does an Rx profile help the underwriter?

It allows him to match up the medications the proposed insured acknowledges taking on the application or during the teleinterview against the actual records.

In this way, it is like cotinine testing in that it pinpoints individuals who do not disclose potentially risk-significant information.

How many insurers currently use these profiles?

It's hard to say for certain because use is increasing rapidly. Likely over 40% of life companies use them routinely at this writing, but there is reason to project that this will increase dramatically in the next 1-2 years.

Why don't all insurers use this?

Chief underwriters only have so many dollars to allocate to screening proposed insureds and they constantly have to assess the relative merits of the alternatives open to them. If they believe that other requirements confer more value, they may abstain from using this or any other requirement.

Has there been any consumer pushback against Rx profile use?

For years, this was not an issue. Then, in August 2008, articles appeared in several major media sources. Some were more balanced in their approach than others, but all of them raised issues concerning the use of these profiles.

It is significant that all of this pushback was directed toward their use in health insurance only. Considering all of the issues being aired about health insurance, it comes as no surprise that the use of the Rx profile would come under fire by persons who do not understand how and why it is used.

As I said, Rx profiles are really no different than cotinine tests. Their predominant role is confirming what is disclosed on the application.

Moreover, in the age of teleunderwriting, the impact of Rx profiles should be mainly positive from the applicant's perspective because they facilitate faster and more favorable decisions.

Motor Vehicle Report (MVR)

What is an MVR?

A report showing the applicant's driving record in his state of residence over a finite period of time.

Do most insurers make use of MVRs in screening?

Probably 80% or more do so, on some basis. MVRs are comparatively inexpensive and are secured far more rapidly than most other requirements.

In which age groupings are MVRs thought to confer the most value?

- Age 25 and under – because adolescent and young adult drivers have the most fatal accidents.
- Age 65 and over – because the incidence of accidents increases at these ages (and for other reasons as well).

Do insurers typically screen all applicants, or at least all in these age groups, with MVRs?

No – most of them have a face amount threshold just like they have with other screening tests. The most prevalent threshold is $100,000 overall, although some companies do not start until a much larger sum is applied for.

Which violations are of greatest concern?

Driving under the influence – variously described as DUI or DWI – is far and away the most significant adverse finding. When you consider that well over 50% of persons convicted of drunk driving are chronic alcohol abusers and/or alcohol-dependent, you appreciate how important this is to insurability.

While most adverse underwriting action due to motor vehicle issues is associated with driving under the influence, we also have concerns when applicants have a large number of moving violations over a short span of time, their licenses are suspended or revoked, they engage in reckless driving and so on.

Bad driving records are a prime example of what we call "risk-taking behaviors" and most deaths under age 40 are directly related to the consequences of these behaviors (accidents, homicides and suicides).

What type of rating is assessed for adverse driving records?

A flat extra premium in the range of $3 to $5 per thousand.

Do potentially insurable cases involving a history of driving under the influence usually lead to additional elective requirements?

In my view, they should, depending on the context of the case.

The CDT alcohol marker is especially appropriate here because a positive test is strongly associated with heavy drinking, and I already mentioned the association between drunk driving and alcohol use disorders.

If the substance involved was a drug of abuse, then screening with the so-called NIDA 5 multidrug test is a worthy consideration.

Another area underwriters should focus in on is any history of injuries or other kind of trauma, often reflected in visits to emergency departments. I encourage them to pay close attention to these situations in all applicants who have histories involving substance abuse and other risk-taking behaviors.

INSPECTION REPORTS

What are inspection reports?

Detailed reports done by specialized service firms, typically interviewing the applicant as well as gathering a range of information including civil and criminal court records, etc.

What is a personal history interview (PHI)?

An inspection-report equivalent, more or less, completed as a telephone interview.

How does a PHI differ from a teleunderwriting interview?

This varies a lot by company and no doubt some use the term PHI in a context that might meet the criteria for being called a teleunderwriting interview. In general, however, these calls do not expand upon YES answers to application questions by asking additional questions (this being the defining distinction of the teleinterview).

Do most insurers use inspection reports/PHIs?

Not any more. Use is declining because of the embrace of teleinterviewing.

Are some inspection reports limited solely to financial information?

Yes, typically for larger amount cases or where there are complexities of a financial nature that bear on the question of the need for the amount of coverage applied for.

Other Potential Screening Requirements

Are there other screening requirements which at least some insurers use routinely at some age/amount of coverage?

Yes.

Virtually all of the so-called "reflexive" requirements may be used to screen by any given company. However, we will cover them under REFLEXIVE REQUIREMENTS because most companies use them in this context rather than to screen routinely.

CHAPTER 5

—•——•——•——•—

Reflexive Requirements

What do we mean by a "reflexive" requirement?

A requirement ordered for one of two main reasons:

- A specific finding on a screening test
- At the underwriter's discretion because of something learned from another requirement

Do all insurers use at least some reflexive requirements in life underwriting?

Yes, although the ones used and the scenarios in which they are used differ very widely.

What are the most commonly used reflexive requirements?

- Glycohemoglobin (HbA1-c)
- Microalbumin
- Hepatitis C test
- Hepatitis B tests
- Alcohol markers

GLYCOHEMOGLOBIN (HBA1-C)

What is glycohemoglobin?

A blood test which reflects one's average blood sugar level over the past 4 to 6+ weeks, expressed as a percentage.

When do underwriters request this test?

On applicants with a history of diabetes as well as those suspected of possibly being diabetic based on findings on the screening blood profile (mainly elevated glucose and/or elevated fructosamine).

Do most insurers use this test?

Yes – certainly 90% or more.

We will discuss HbA1-c in more detail in conjunction with diabetes further on.

MICROALBUMIN (MA)

What is the microalbumin test?

A rather precise measurement of the amount of albumin protein in the urine.

Why do underwriters use it?

Because it is a major enhancement over testing for urine protein.

Albumin is the main protein in the urine but there are others as well. With one rare exception (related to a cancer known as multiple myeloma), the other proteins have little or no significance. It is the quantity of albumin in the urine that matters. Therefore, by doing the microalbumin test on persons who screen positive* for protein in the urine (proteinuria), we can distinguish those that may matter from the rest.

* "Positive" is the word used when a test shows the findings that it was used to try to detect, in a certain minimum quantity. Conversely, when a test is deemed "negative," this means either that nothing is found or the amount detected is so minimal that it does not matter.

Do most insurers use MA as a reflexive test?

At this time, the majority of insurers do (and the rest should).

Most of the time, the laboratory they use for their testing has standing orders from them to run the MA test if proteinuria is detected at some threshold amount. At other times, the underwriter orders the MA electively even if the urine protein screening test was negative.

In which contexts are most MA tests done?

- Protein in the screening urine test
- Elevated glucose, fructosamine or glycosylated hemoglobin (HbA1-c) test
- Known or suspected diabetes
- Known or suspected prediabetes
- History of kidney disease
- History of high blood pressure or elevated BP readings on the current paramedical

The first three are pretty much "standard operating procedure" for most insurers that use MA.

Does MA testing have any value which is not yet widely recognized as a reason to use it in underwriting?

You bet.

It is a first class cardiovascular disease risk marker, as good if not better than most all of the ones we now use routinely.

HEPATITIS B AND C TESTS

What is the test for hepatitis C?

It's an antibody test designated anti-HCV.

If you have a positive anti-HCV test, it means you were – and likely still are – infected with this virus. About 4 out of 5 people who test positive are still infected and we say they have chronic hepatitis C. The other 20% probably have cleared the virus from their body but continue to have antibodies against the virus.

Is there any way to tell which of those who test positive for the HCV antibodies remain infected?

Yes, but the test needed to do this is too expensive for insurance purposes. If someone is said to have a positive hepatitis C antibody test based on insurance screening and they do not already know they have chronic hepatitis C, they need to check this out with their doctor.

Is anti-HCV a blood test?

Yes.

Do most insurers use this anti-HCV test?

Yes, when there are reasons to suspect possible hepatitis C infection.

We will discuss this in more depth when we review hepatitis C as an insurance risk further on.

Do any companies screen for hepatitis C?

Yes, and the number doing so is growing because the word is that the "pay-off" from screening is significant.

What is the main reason companies screen with the anti-HCV test?

Because as many as 50% of persons infected who apply for insurance have normal liver enzymes and hence would not be detected without screening.

Is the hepatitis B test similar to the one for hepatitis C?

Yes and no (classic underwriter answer, eh?).

Yes – the hepatitic test protocol includes antibody tests, depending on which components are used.

No – the two primary tests we use for hepatitis B are antigen, not antibody, tests. Antigen tests detect the virus itself whereas antibody tests only detect proteins called antibodies which the person's own immune system has manufactured to fight the virus infection.

What are the two hepatitis B tests mainly used in insurance?

- Hepatitis B surface antigen, designated HBsAg
- Hepatitis B "e" antigen, designated HBeAg

The surface antigen detects the presence of the virus.

If the virus is present, the "e" antigen test is done to determine if the virus is actively reproducing (as opposed to latent) and thus at higher risk for leading to liver damage.

Do most insurers do hepatitis B reflexive testing?

Yes – but the criteria they use differ considerably.

Do any insurers screen with hepatitis B tests?

Only a few in the US; screening for hepatitis B is considerably more prevalent in Canada.

There will be more on hepatitis B further on when we look at it as an impairment.

ALCOHOL MARKERS

What are alcohol markers?

Tests used specifically to determine if someone consumes very large amounts of alcohol.

Is this the same as testing for "alcohol abuse" and "alcoholism"?

No. You cannot conclude that a positive alcohol marker test means either abuse or dependency (alcoholism). All it tells us is that the applicant drinks heavily.

What are the alcohol markers currently in use in underwriting as reflexive tests?

- Carbohydrate deficient transferrin (CDT)
- Hemoglobin-associated aldehyde (HAA)

Are they blood tests?

Yes.

Which one is used more often?

CDT accounts for 90%+ of alcohol marker testing at this time.

Why?

CDT is much better known in clinical medicine and is FDA approved. A great deal has been written about it, and the quality of CDT test methods has steadily improved over the last 10+ years. It is also used in law enforcement.

By comparison, the HAA test is virtually unknown clinically and is rarely done, to my knowledge, in any context besides insurance.

Do all insurers use alcohol markers on some basis?

No – there have been some that have refrained despite the fact that a clear majority use one or both of these markers on some basis.

Why do some companies not use alcohol markers?

You'd have to ask them to know for sure, but I'm sure a good bit of it has to do with concerns with what the tests do and do not tell us.

How reliable are these tests?

In the context in which we use them – ordering them when we already have reason to believe the proposed insured might be using alcohol to excess – they are quite reliable.

That is, with a major caveat pertaining to the CDT test.

What is the caveat?

The #1 reason why underwriters order alcohol marker tests is because of elevation of the GGT test on the screening blood profile.

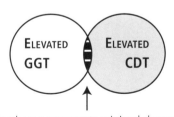

Striped area represents minimal degree of overlap where GGT and CDT are both elevated

GGT and CDT both detect heavy drinking. But, each is better at detecting a particular subset of heavy drinkers. CDT is more prone to elevate in persons who drink to excess daily, whereas GGT is better for detecting persons who binge drink.

The problem is that elevated GGT and elevated CDT do not overlap very often in the same person.

What inference can we make from this?

The majority of persons who test positive for GGT will have a negative CDT and vice versa.

In some clinical settings, experts recommend using GGT and CDT together to screen for heavy drinking, rather than using CDT as we often do (to try to confirm whether a positive GGT test is really due to too much drinking).

Until such time as this problem is "fixed" with a better testing option, it really makes no sense – at least to me – to order a CDT test on someone who has an ISOLATED elevated GGT test.

Is HAA a better test to resolve the significance of an elevated GGT?

One study, done in the 1990s, showed that it definitely was.

Is there a delay when the underwriter orders CDT or HAA?

No – provided it is done within a month of the time the blood is collected, so the lab still has the original blood specimen to test.

Do any insurers test for blood alcohol?

Yes, but we cannot see any value in doing so.

Are there any new alcohol markers on the horizon?

Yes.

There has been increasing reference in some quarters to a test known as ethyl glucuronide (EtG). This test is said to have a potential intermediary role between screening with liver enzymes and reflexively testing with CDT.

We looked at the pros and cons of EtG based on the worldwide medical literature in mid-2008 and, unless there have been major developments enhancing its value in the interim, the need for using this test in underwriting is, at best, dubious.

Other Reflexive Tests

Are there any other reflexive tests which insurers use more than rarely?

Yes.

Some are uncommonly used and their use is unlikely to increase (for good reasons). Others are what you might call "up and coming" test alternatives, which could be used to screen or as "reflex tests," and perhaps ideally as both.

Which of these are worth knowing about at this time?

- NT-proBNP
- Hemoglobin
- Cystatin C
- hs-CRP
- Carcinoembryonic antigen (CEA)
- Skin cholesterol test

NT-proBNP

What is NT-proBNP?

A relatively new blood test for cardiac impairments.

Can it be done on the same blood sample collected to run a routine screening blood profile?

Yes.

Is it being used by insurers at this time?

Yes, and the number continues to increase. Count on NT-proBNP becoming a major insurance test in the near future.

Why?

Elevated blood levels correlate so well with heart abnormalities that this test should eventually replace screening with resting and exercise (treadmill) ECGs.

Does an elevated NT-proBNP test mean that the insured is seriously ill and needs medical intervention?

In the absence of symptoms or other major findings, no...so it does not convey the same message inherent in a tumor marker test.

NT-proBNP tells us that there is sufficient mortality and morbidity risk to justify taking underwriting action based on the test's results.

Should a person who has an elevated NT-proBNP test see their physician?

Personally, I think anybody who has any unexpected elevated lab test that is sufficiently significant to result in us taking adverse underwriting action should always get the results to their doctor and ask for his clinical opinion regarding how it pertains to their ongoing health care.

Has much been written about NT-proBNP for insurers?

I did a mammoth white paper on this test – published at www. hankgeorgeinc.com – examining all of the underwriting implications which I could discern at the time the paper was written. Since it was published, there have been many more studies which extend the favorable implications of NT-proBNP in our context. We may have to do an updated NT-proBNP paper soon.

In early 2007, there was an excellent paper by a veteran medical director in the *Journal of Insurance Medicine* which further underscored the underwriting potential for this test.

What is holding NT-proBNP back?

The inherently conservative nature of the industry, and a bit of pushback from certain parties, largely for reasons that would wilt in the face of all the demonstrated advantages.

Unless something comes to be known that limits the applicability of NT-proBNP as a screening test in underwriting, there are no sound reasons why it should not be used widely at older ages.

Hemoglobin

What is hemoglobin?

The protein which transports oxygen in the bloodstream.

Can it be tested for in a blood sample collected by a paramedical technician?

Yes, and relatively inexpensively as well.

When is an abnormal hemoglobin test significant in underwriting?

- When it is below the normal range, this is the same as saying the person is anemic and then it is up to the personal physician to decide if that anemia is significant enough, in context, to further evaluate.
- When it is above normal – which is far less common – it may mean the person has too many red blood cells for some reason. If I had an elevated hemoglobin reading, you can bet I would get it evaluated by a doctor.

Is there sufficient value, from an underwriting perspective, in screening with hemoglobin?

Some say yes and do it; a few tried it and don't do it any longer; most have never evaluated it in our context.

My intuition tells me this could have substantial value as a screening test at older ages because of the risk implications of anemia from late middle-age onwards.

Cystatin C

What is cystatin C?

A relatively new blood test intended for clinical use in detecting persons with kidney damage, much like creatinine (only better).

Is it being used in underwriting?

Not at this time, although the industry labs do make it available.

Is there any reason to think it may catch on?

Yes.

In fact, my brand new white paper on cystatin C's pros and cons as an underwriting screening asset was just published and is available at www.hankgeorgeinc.com.

Cystatin C appears to have value in important ways beyond "just" kidney function. It now looks like Cystatin C could have a definite place alongside NT-proBNP when it comes to a viable alternative to some of the baggage-ridden things we do now.

hs-**CRP**

What is hs-CRP?

A blood test related to inflammation. It is also called simply CRP.

Is it being used in underwriting?

A few companies probably use it in some context. There are pros and cons connected with this test in our context and it has yet to catch on with most insurers as a screening test.

CEA

What is carcinoembryonic antigen (CEA)?

A tumor marker, tested for with blood and used in clinical medicine, primarily in the context of known or suspected colon cancer.

Is it used clinically as a screening test in a way similar to PSA?

No – with good reason.

Do any insurers use CEA to screen proposed insureds at this time?

Yes, but not many.

Do you think it will be used more in the future?

No...and I hope I'm right because I have concerns about screening for cancer with a test that is not used in this context in health care!

SKIN CHOLESTEROL TEST

What is the skin cholesterol test?

As the name suggests, it is a test that involves measuring cholesterol from a skin-related process.

The proper name for it is the "skin sterol test" and it is marketed using the brand name PREVU®.

How does it work?

A pad is placed on the palm of the hand, pulled off and then sent in for laboratory analysis.

Is it painful?

Not at all. Probably the easiest test we could ever do!

Does it give a true reading of one's cholesterol?

Not in the same sense as the blood cholesterol test...but, when you compare the blood cholesterol test to the skin cholesterol test, the evidence is pretty good that the skin test more closely correlates with the risk of significant coronary disease.

Is it being used in underwriting at this time?

As I write this, no. However, there is reason to believe this may change in the next 12-24 months.

What would encourage insurers to consider screening with skin cholesterol testing?

- It is incredibly easy to do and would be readily amenable to producer-mediated collection on the same basis as oral fluid.
- It is more customer-friendly than any test we have access to.
- It has a better correlation with risk than blood cholesterol.

What might discourage its use?

Certainly the cost will be a big factor, as well as where it is deemed to fit into the screening process. Remember, our blood test limits are set fairly low at older ages and there is no way that the skin cholesterol test can offset the value of the entire blood profile.

Final Thoughts on Testing

Has testing in insurance – looking at its net impact in a broad sense – been to the advantage of your clients?

I think it has.

This is what two authors said about the subject in *The Lancet*, a major British medical journal, in 2004:

> "...despite the introduction of innumerable screening, diagnostic and therapeutic technologies over the past century, the percentage of people who have been able to obtain life insurance has in fact risen."

Nick Raithatha and Richard D. Smith
The Lancet
363(2004);395

These authors were, of course, speaking more broadly than just about screening tests we use, but the fact is that for every case that is adversely influenced by screening there are undoubtedly several which can be insured more favorably because the test was done and was normal.

Another advantage is that insurance screening sometimes initiates a sequence of events that leads to diagnosis and treatment of an unsuspected illness before the proposed insured's well-being is jeopardized.

I've personally been involved in dozens of these cases over the years and could tell you stories that would grab and hold your attention.

CHAPTER 6

—•——•——•——•—

Tobacco Use; Tobacco and Drug Testing

In what ways do people consume tobacco?

Smoke
- Cigarettes
- Cigars
- Cigarillos
- Pipes
- Bidis (unfiltered; resemble cigarettes and also called "beedies")
- Kreteks (clove cigarettes)
- Water pipe (hookah, shisha, narghile)

Not Smoked
- Snuff
- Chewing tobacco
- Mixed with other substances, such as betel

Why is the subject of tobacco use so significant to insurability?

Because cigarette smoking – the overwhelmingly most common mode of tobacco consumption – is the #1 preventable cause of excess mortality and morbidity.

It has been estimated that male "coffin nail" addicts lose 13 years of life expectancy, whereas female cigarette devotees sacrifice 14.5 years of their time on earth.

In addition, the risk of disability is at least 50% higher in current smokers.

CIGARETTES

How many North Americans smoke cigarettes?

Among adults, roughly 19% of women and 24% of men.

What else do we know about the distribution of cigarette smokers?

- The % of users dropped like a stone between 1965 and 1995, but has leveled off now.
- It decreases steeply with years of education, especially in those with more than 12 years of formal education.
- The same is true, albeit less dramatically, in terms of income.
- It is only 1/3rd as common at ages 65 and over as it is in younger persons.

In terms of mortality and morbidity, what factor related to cigarette smoking stands out like the proverbial "sore thumb"?

Pack-years of consumption, which is the number of years of smoking multiplied by number of packs smoked per day.

In other words, if someone has smoked 25 years and smokes 2 packs a day, they have 50 pack-years under their belt. If they'd smoked the same number of years but only consumed half a pack each day, they'd have 12.5 pack-years (which equates to only 25% as much cumulative exposure).

Why are pack-years so pivotal?

Because nearly all health consequences from cigarette smoking are driven by cumulative exposure rather than current use.

Do insurers make use of pack-years in underwriting?

Very few, which is disappointing because this could be easily done by asking just 2 more questions!

Are there other insurability issues related to being a cigarette smoker?

Yes, two, and both insidious:

- Heavy smokers are far more likely to be heavy drinkers.
- Cigarette smoking is a marker for many other kinds of "risk-taking behaviors" as well.

Cigars

Is the use of cigars increasing?

Yes, since the 1990s. It started as a manifestation of "yuppie flu" but has become more widespread in all population segments.

Recent American Lung Association statistics say it's up 9% in recent years (14% in women) and highest at ages 25-44.

Do cigar smokers have excess mortality and morbidity?

Overall, without a doubt.

However, it is far lower than in cigarette smokers, especially those who have never smoked cigarettes on a regular basis.

In a 1999 study published in *The New England Journal of Medicine*, there was a huge difference in risk of disease depending upon how many cigars were consumed per day. Those who smoked 5 or more had anywhere from a 25% to a 5-fold higher risk, depending upon the impairment.

The American Cancer Society's Cancer Prevention Study I pretty much exonerated 1-2/day cigar consumption where mortality is concerned.

A celebrated ongoing study of physicians found no increased mortality in current or past cigar smokers.

What factors probably account for lower mortality in cigar smokers as compared to cigarette users?

- Most cigar smokers do not inhale; they don't need to because nicotine from cigar smoke is readily absorbed without inhaling.
- Many don't smoke every day (especially the "fad" crowd); even those that do tend to have a far lower lifetime volume of exposure to tobacco toxins as compared to cigarette smokers.
- Most of the fad cigar aficionados are not prior regular cigarette smokers.
- Fad cigar smoking has found a home with a more educated, higher income user group, undoubtedly conferring additional advantages in contrast to the risk-taking behaviors linked to cigarette "narcosis."

PIPES

How common is pipe smoking?

It dropped from 14% in 1965 to 2% 26 years later and remains quite low as compared to cigarettes and cigars. No faddism here.

The vast majority of pipe smokers are middle-aged men but there has been some increase in indulgence in adolescents as well as among women. Pipe users also tend to be better educated and not as disposed to heavy drinking as cigarette addicts.

What is the one factor that raises our eyebrows about pipe smokers, as compared to cigar smokers?

Pipe smoking predisposes to inhaling.

SMOKELESS TOBACCO

Is smokeless use increasing?

It did big time in the 1970s, tripling between 1972 and 1991, with user rates stabilizing from the mid-1990s onward.

What do we know about the distribution of smokeless users?

- Males predominate but female use increased dramatically in the 90s.
- 9% of college men and 8% of male high school students use it.
- As in cigarettes, use is far higher in those with 12 years or less of formal education.
- In 2003, over 1 in 3 professional baseball players indulged.

What are the four main forms of smokeless?

- Moist snuff, which accounts for nearly all of the rise in use and ranks #1.
- Chewing tobacco, which is declining in prevalence.
- Dry snuff, which is the most harmful mode and rapidly in decline.
- The so-called "tobacco lozenge," which must not be confused with the tobacco-free nicotine lozenge used in attempts to quit smoking.

Is tobacco lozenge use on the rise?

Yes, "thanks" to tobacco manufacturers. The "up side" here is that these lozenges contain the lowest levels of carcinogens of any tobacco products.

Is there increased mortality and morbidity in smokeless tobacco use?

If we exclude dry snuff, the answer is still yes, but the magnitude is very modest when contrasted to smoking.

One can't help but take note of major studies which found little if any mortality linked to smokeless use...

...that is, once smokeless users who were current or past cigarette smokers were excluded.

Do cigarette smokers switch to smokeless in an effort to quit?

All the time. And it works far more effectively than any other "quitting aid" on the market.

> *"We find that if all current male smokers began using smokeless tobacco, life years for the current population of adult males in the United States could be extended by approximately 18 million years."*
>
> R. W. Ault, et al.
> *Applied Economics*
> 36(2004):17

Not everybody, of course, agrees that going from cigarettes to smokeless is a worthy goal that should be officially sanctioned. Clearly, no tobacco is best.

Alternative Methods of Tobacco Consumption

What are the four dominant "alternative methods" of tobacco use?

- Bidis (Beedies)
- Kreteks (clove cigarettes)
- Water pipe (hookah, shisha, margile)
- Betel

What needs to be said about the first three?

- Their use isn't nearly as common as cigarettes, cigars or smoke-less tobacco, but their users are in sufficient numbers that we see routinely as proposed insureds (even if we don't always know it when it happens!).
- All three are at least as bad if not worse than cigarette smoking in terms of exposure to carcinogens and other harmful substances.
- There is no justification for underwriting them one bit more favorably than cigarette smokers, based on my review of the world literature for all three.
- Most insurers do not ask – specifically, by name – about any of them, which could foster nondisclosure (despite the fact that most insurers do ask about "tobacco use in any form").

Betel

What is betel?

The wrong name for an addicting, carcinogenic plant product which is properly called "areca nut." It is widely consumed in India, Pakistan, Taiwan, and throughout Southeast Asia, and also by immigrants from those regions.

Does betel contain tobacco?

No – but, tobacco is often consumed with betel.

It there excess mortality and morbidity associated with betel use?

Yes, in most forms when used on a regular basis like smokeless tobacco.

However, in some forms – supari, for example, which is consumed as a food – I haven't seen evidence that there's any increase in risk.

Do most insurers ask about betel use?

Not in the US, based on a 2007 survey.

Should they?

Yes. And distinguish how it is consumed as well.

Tobacco Use Underwriting

When did insurers start making distinctions between users and non-users in how insurance products are priced?

In the 1970s, fueled by studies done by several proactive carriers.

Has our approach to tobacco use changed in the interim?

Dramatically:

As you can see from this diagram, we went through 4 distinct iterations of "smoker/user" underwriting, each more broad than the last.

We started with "cigarettes only," then added all forms of smoking, all forms of tobacco and finally any nicotine use, in that order.

What will happen in the years ahead?

There are several possibilities, including standing pat or backtracking, so to speak, by removing one or more elements from the current definition.

Given all of the evidence at hand, the most logical candidate for repositioning is oral tobacco use in persons who have never been regular cigarette smokers.

Do all insurers adhere to the "all forms of tobacco and nicotine use = 'user' " definition?

No.

Some do not include oral tobacco in their definition. Others make exceptions for "occasional" (celebratory) cigar use or treat use of nicotine products differently from tobacco use.

What is the "fly in the ointment" if we were to wish to move away from "all tobacco and nicotine use" in favor of a less all-encompassing "user" definition?

The difference between "user" and "non-user" premiums seems to be sufficient incentive for some proposed insureds to develop a sudden case of "amnesia" during the application process.

With the "all tobacco and nicotine use" definition, we prevent this deception from succeeding because:

- We screen with cotinine.
- Cotinine is positive in all forms of tobacco and nicotine use.

Therefore, no matter whether they have "smoker's amnesia" or "user's amnesia," we will find out with the cotinine test!

However, if we decided – for example – to exclude oral tobacco from our definition, the role of cotinine testing would be compromised.

Why?

If a prevaricating cigarette smoker claimed instead that he was a snuff user, a positive cotinine test could no longer be deemed to prove he wasn't telling the truth.

Cotinine is present in both cigarette smokers and snuff users!

COTININE TESTING

What is cotinine?

A byproduct of nicotine and the substance we test for in insurance screening.

Will anyone who uses tobacco have cotinine in their bodily fluids?

Yes, because all tobacco products contain nicotine…and where there's nicotine, there's going to be cotinine, soon after the nicotine is ingested.

Do most North American insurers test for cotinine?

I am not aware of any carrier that does not test for cotinine in either urine or oral fluid on individually underwritten life, disability or critical illness insurance. I would also expect that LTC and health insurers who do any lab testing would include cotinine as well.

How long can we detect cotinine after last use of nicotine?

It all depends on how much nicotine was absorbed, how long ago it was consumed and other factors such as the subject's state of hydration, etc.

Given these caveats, the answer is anywhere from 1 to 7 days, with the average being right around 3-4 days.

Which means that if someone completely abstained from all tobacco and nicotine intake for a week, the odds of them testing positive would be virtually nil under ordinary circumstances.

This fact, however, must be tempered by another major consideration: individuals found to have misrepresented their tobacco use status have not fared well when insurers have contested the policy or a claim. Before anyone contemplates trying to "beat the system" through a period of transient abstinence, they need to consider this long and hard.

Does the level of cotinine help any in this distinction?

Not at all.

Knowing the level of cotinine only has value in terms of the threshold set to distinguish nicotine users from non-users. Once the level exceeds that threshold, it is utterly meaningless to underwriters.

Why?

Because the factors that determine a nicotine user's cotinine level have little to do with the mode of use. They are driven by volume of use within a window period of a few days, which in turn is greatly influenced by state of hydration (how much water they have in their body) and other factors as well.

On any given day, a smokeless user could have as high or higher a cotinine level than a 2-pack-a-day smoker.

If it were up to me, insurance laboratories would not report actual cotinine readings. Their reports would only say "positive" (at or above the threshold) or "negative" (undetectable or detectable only below the threshold). This is all the underwriter needs to know.

What is the threshold for a positive cotinine test?

It varies between companies. They can ask their lab to set the threshold where they are most comfortable.

Can passive exposure to environmental tobacco smoke (ETS) cause a positive cotinine test?

Yes, but only at levels far below the lowest threshold used by any insurer to define a positive test.

After reading everything I could find in the world medical literature pertaining to cotinine testing, I must conclude that it is IMPOSSIBLE for ETS exposure to result in a positive insurance cotinine screening test.

Don't even bother bringing it up!

Are there other substances that also cause some amount of cotinine to be detected in the testing process?

Yes.

We know, for example, that some vegetables contain nicotine, as do certain insecticides and herbicides. However, the levels resulting from these exposures are tiny and will not cause a positive cotinine test.

Do the nicotine patch and nicotine gum cause a positive cotinine screening test?

They can and often do, because they contain nicotine and nicotine begets cotinine after ingestion.

Is this true for all products used in quitting smoking?

No – only those that contain nicotine. At this writing, this would include the nicotine:

- Patch
- Gum
- Nasal spray
- Inhaler
- Lozenge

There are medications used in quitting smoking – such as the anti-depressant bupropion – that do not contain nicotine and therefore would never test positive.

Is it possible for a person to have a positive insurance cotinine test due to use of nicotine for reasons other than tobacco consumption or quitting the habit?

Yes. The nicotine patch has been used successfully in the treatment of a number of disorders:

- Attention-deficit hyperactivity disorder (ADHD)
- Parkinson disease
- Tourette syndrome
- Ulcerative colitis

It is imperative that anyone using the nicotine patch for reasons other than quitting tobacco use disclose this fact during medical-history taking and also indicate specifically why the nicotine patch is being used.

Do any insurers test for cotinine under age 18?

Yes, as I was surprised to learn recently.

Why surprised?

Imagine a scenario where a kid is sneaking around smoking behind his parents' back and gets "caught" by virtue of a cotinine test!

How many proposed insureds test positive for cotinine overall?

In 2006 data from Heritage Laboratories, 12.2% were positive (8.8% of females and 14.6% of males).

Why is this number only half of the percentage of cigarette smokers (not to mention other nicotine users) in the general population?

Because tobacco use is much more common in persons with less education and lower socioeconomic status…and they buy far less life and health insurance at cotinine screening thresholds than those with more education and higher incomes.

When we look at positive cotinine levels by face amount, this becomes clear.

Face Amount	Cotinine Positive
< $100,000	16.5%
$100,000	15.7%
$100,001-$499,000	12.3%
$500,000 or more	7.3%

Heritage Labs. 2006 Data.

Cotinine Positive Rates Ranked In Order			
Highest Six		Lowest Six	
Guam	33.4%	Puerto Rico	6.0%
Mississippi	21.2%	Hawaii	6.4%
West Virginia	19.3%	Utah	6.4%
Oklahoma	19.3%	California	7.0%
Louisiana	18.9%	Connecticut	8.0%
Alabama	18.9%	New York	8.3%

Heritage Labs. 2006 Data.

Cotinine positives also differ significantly by age grouping (highest at ages 40-49; lowest over age 60), and by state or territory of residence.

Are there ever false-positive* cotinine screening tests?

I investigated this subject in 2007 at the behest of several clients.

One industry lab said it had no false-positives and produced credible data in support of this statement (which I personally reviewed).

The other labs report rare cases of apparent false-positives when they retest specimens that tested cotinine-positive on screening, using the best confirmation test available.

This may have something to do with screening test methods.

Either way, underwriters, producers and proposed insureds should be confident that when this test is positive in industry labs, nicotine ingestion is virtually certain.

* "False-positive" means that the test is positive but the cause of the positive result is not the reason for which the test was done. Virtually all tests will inevitably result in at least some false-positives.

Are there false-negative* cotinine screening tests?

Sure, all the time.

For example, if a smoker has a bad cold and cuts way back or stops entirely for a few days (while drinking lots of fluids), a test done before he resumes his usual tobacco dose could show a quantity of cotinine below the positive threshold.

Years ago, we did an experiment where we asked non-smokers to smoke one cigar without inhaling. Only one had a minimally positive cotinine test, which tells us that occasional non-inhaling cigar smokers are unlikely to test positive.

No doubt this is also true for many light users of oral tobacco and persons using nicotine-based aids to quit smoking.

But – this is the insurer's worry, not yours! Your client, assuming normal mental health status, is unlikely to claim he uses nicotine when in fact he doesn't!

* "False negative" means the test is negative but the person tested used the substance; in this case, tobacco or a nicotine product.

Do we have any way of distinguishing between tobacco smoking and oral tobacco use?

Yes, a blood test called thiocyanate.

I investigated this subject and unfortunately most studies are pretty old. What I did find, however, is both good news and bad news:

- Good news: it appears that over 80% of persons using oral tobacco only could be distinguished from tobacco smokers with a thiocyanate test.
- Bad news: there is some evidence that thiocyanate levels can be raised by certain commonly consumed vegetables. This could result in false-positives and mislead the underwriter into thinking the proposed insured smokes when he does not.

Before thiocyanate is used in underwriting, the issue of false-positives from various foods needs to be resolved. If this turns out okay, then thiocyanate could play a role in helping oral tobacco users avoid the appearance of being smokers.

What should I do if my client denies any form of nicotine use and has a positive cotinine test?

1. Level with him and explain that the odds of the test being wrong are tiny to nil.
2. Review all of the causes of positive cotinine tests (as shown in this chapter) with him, because there is a chance that one of them may explain the discrepancy.
3. Understand that the most likely explanation by far – considering

the quality of insurance tests and the high thresholds set for a positive – is nondisclosure of tobacco or nicotine use on the part of the client.

DRUGS OF ABUSE TESTING

Which drug is most widely tested for in underwriting?

Cocaine – by a huge margin.

Do all insurers test for cocaine?

In the 2007 Underwriting Requirements Survey, 94% reported doing age/amount urine cocaine testing, and no doubt some that do not have cocaine in their urine profile nevertheless test for it with oral fluid.

Why cocaine?

Because it is – or at least was – the most widely used, highly risk-significant drug of abuse among life and health insurance seekers.

What do you mean by "or at least was"?

There is evidence that methamphetamine abuse is now more wide-spread overall and may soon rival cocaine use among insurance buyers.

Do insurers test for methamphetamine?

Probably 1 in 10, but that number is likely to increase.

Do insurers test for marijuana?

In the aforementioned survey, 18% said they did, but it wasn't specified that they screen with marijuana tests, and I would think screening for marijuana would be uncommon.

If they didn't screen with the marijuana test, how were they using it?

Most likely it would be ordered when the underwriter was suspicious about possible drug abuse for some other reason.

Are there other drugs that insurers test for?

A few insurers require what is called the "NIDA 5," consisting of:

- Marijuana
- Cocaine
- Opiates (heroin, etc.)
- Methamphetamine
- Phencyclidine ("angel dust")

Maybe one or two others do opiate testing in addition to cocaine.

In what substances can drugs of abuse be tested for?

- Blood
- Urine
- Oral fluid
- Hair
- Sweat
- Toenails

How widespread is toenail testing in insurance?

Zero – and I can't foresee anyone asking paramedical technicians to start using nail clippers!

We used to do drug-related hair testing but that is seldom requested any longer.

Our two drug testing modalities are urine and oral fluid, in that order.

Do we make our decisions based on screening tests?

No – that is unthinkable considering that the overall false-positive rate is probably around 5%.

All positive drug screening tests performed for North American insurers are confirmed as truly positive, using state-of-the-art science, before they are reported as positive by the lab to the insurer.

What confirmation test is used?

Almost always what we call the "gold standard" in drug confirmation: gas chromatography with mass spectrometry (abbreviated GC-MS).

Do we take any steps with urine testing to detect tampering for the purpose of concealing drug use?

Yes, we check four things:

- The temperature of the specimen – as soon as the applicant gives it to the paramedical technician – to make sure it was voided by a living mammal.
- The pH (degree of acidity) of the urine, to "red flag" contaminants.
- The urinary creatinine concentration, to make sure it is urine.
- The specific gravity, to see if the specimen was "watered down."

Drug screening has become very sophisticated!

How long can the drugs we test for be detected in a urine specimen?

The "window period" for both cocaine and methamphetamine is 2 to 4 days. But, again, there are extenuating circumstances where that interval can be considerably longer.

Marijuana, on the other hand, can be detected as long as 30 days after last use.

Why this huge difference?

Cocaine and methamphetamine are water-soluble and hence pass quickly through the system. Marijuana is not water-soluble and takes much longer to process out and excrete.

Do we test for cocaine itself?

No.

We test for a byproduct (called a metabolite). In cocaine, the metabolite is benzoylecgonine.

How often do proposed insureds test positive for cocaine?

According to the latest (2006) data we received from Heritage Labs, the overall confirmed positive rate is 2.2 per 1000 (2.9 in males and 1.3 in females).

Do cocaine positive rates vary by face amounts?

Yes, the detection rate at < $100,000 is 5 times higher than it is at $100,001-$400,000.

The highest incidence of positives in both genders is at ages 40-49. In men, the positive rate over age 60 is less than 25% of that reported in middle-aged guys.

Are positives for cocaine most prevalent in the same states as posititives for cotinine?

No.

I won't be citing the data here, but suffice it to say that Puerto Rico, as an example, goes from last in cotinine to first in cocaine, followed by South Carolina, Delaware, Florida and the District of Columbia. Utah has the lowest cocaine detection rate, followed by Oklahoma and Idaho.

Has the cocaine-positive rate been decreasing in recent years?

Yes, from 5.4/1,000 in 2002 to 2.2/1,000 in 2006.

This decline is consistent with the drop in cocaine use in the general population.

What is the main cause of confirmed-positive cocaine screening tests among proposed insureds?

Cocaine use as a drug of abuse in 99+% of cases.

How can you be so sure?

Because there are essentially no false-positives with GC-MS confirmation, and the positive tests due to cocaine ingestion on any basis except drug abuse are rarely encountered.

What are the possible causes of a positive cocaine test which are not associated with drug abuse?

- Certain "herbal" teas, primarily manufactured in South America, contain small amounts of coca, the plant product from which cocaine is derived.
- Very rarely, topical anesthesia will contain cocaine (which, as users know, has a notable numbing effect!). The physician may or may not advise the patient of this.

How can we be confident that these explanations rarely apply in the context of insurance screening?

Importation of cocaine-laced herbal tea is illegal.

Cocaine-based anesthesia, as I said, is rarely used anymore except in one surgical procedure: nasal septoplasty. In this setting, cocaine is administered by inserting a drug-dipped sponge into the nostrils. One would think most surgeons would disclose the fact that cocaine has been used.

What can the proposed insured do if he is found to have a positive cocaine insurance test and believes it was due to anesthesia?

He should provide contact information for the surgeon, and this shouldn't be a problem since the surgery had to be just a couple of days prior to the collection of the urine or oral fluid specimen.

Then, the underwriter can confirm the facts with that physician.

What about that new energy drink called "Cocaine Energy Drink"?

It doesn't contain any cocaine.

Don't poppy seeds cause a positive cocaine test?

No. It is theoretically possible (but extremely unlikely) that they could cause a positive test for opiates, heroin, etc.

Can the lab determine if a positive heroin screening test was caused by poppy seed ingestion?

Yes, using a confirmation test…so it is beyond improbable that poppy seed consumption will have any underwriting consequences!

Can one get a false-positive methamphetamine test from substances chemically related to methamphetamine?

For the record, these would mainly be amphetamine-based stimulants as well as ecstasy and drugs similar to it.

The answer is YES and NO.

Yes – positive screening tests are possible.

No – positive methamphetamine confirmation tests only occur with methamphetamine use.

Have you heard any creative explanations for positive cocaine tests?

Yes. Recently someone alleged that they tested positive from handling currency frequently. This argument was based on the fact that traces of cocaine are not uncommon on paper money.

The "problem" is that the amount is so tiny that the screening test will not register it. This said, I would discourage "intimate contact" with $20 bills just as a precaution!

CHAPTER 7

—●—●—●—●—

Liver Tests

Why devote a whole chapter to just liver tests?

Because since insurers started doing routine blood profile screening 30-some years ago, no tests have generated as much controversy as the liver-related tests on these profiles.

Why?

Two main reasons:

- The stark difference between how these tests are perceived in insurance underwriting as compared to clinical medicine.
- Insufficient knowledge about these tests on the part of many clinical doctors.

What are the liver-related tests?

- Gamma-glutamyltransferase (GGT, GGTP)
- Alanine aminotransferase (ALT, SGPT)
- Aspartate aminotransferase (AST, SGOT)
- Alkaline phosphatase (ALP, AP)
- Total bilirubin

Is there one in particular where most of the controversy is focused?

Yes – GGT.

But before we get to GGT and the issues surrounding it, let's look briefly at the other four liver-related tests.

Which two are pretty much "cut and dried" and hence unlikely to spark much disagreement?

- Alkaline phosphatase (ALP, AP)
- Bilirubin

Why?

The clinical and insurance perspectives are more or less in alignment.

Alkaline phosphatase is the least likely of the 5 tests to be elevated and, when it is, most cases can be resolved when the degree of elevation is considered in context with other tests and the medical history.

Isolated elevation of total bilirubin in a proposed insured who has no history or other findings associated with liver problems is usually due to a harmless condition known as Gilbert syndrome. Therefore, we usually underwrite isolated mild-to-moderate elevations fairly liberally.

On the other hand, when bilirubin is elevated and there are other lab abnormalities, or the medical history is suspicious for liver-related problems, we take a more conservative approach. In some cases we have no choice but to postpone further underwriting until clinical assessment is done. Fortunately, these cases are fairly rare.

What do you mean by "isolated"?

Isolated, in this setting, means you have one elevated liver test with no other relevant abnormal findings on the blood profile, in the medical history or in the other requirements.

Depending upon which test and how elevated it is, whether or not the elevation is isolated can greatly influence underwriting action.

What are ALT and AST?

The two "liver tests" worthy of being called "liver enzymes," because:

- Like alkaline phosphatase and GGT, they are enzymes.
- Unlike alkaline phosphatase and GGT, the significant ALT and AST elevations we encounter in underwriting invariably involve something related to the liver.

What are the three most common causes of ALT?

- Potentially significant: nonalcoholic fatty liver disease
- Always insignificant: strenuous exercise with muscle trauma

What are the three most common causes of AST?

- Always significant: heavy alcohol intake
- Always insignificant: strenuous exercise with muscle trauma

What if both are elevated?

Then – unless it is due to, once again, "strenuous exercise with muscle trauma" –the answer sometimes depends on the ratio of the two tests. This ratio, aptly named the "AST-to-ALT ratio," is important because:

- If greater than 1 (especially 2 or higher), significant liver damage (frequently but not necessarily due to alcohol) looms large as a possible cause.
- If less than 1, liver damage may be present but it is unlikely to be due to alcohol and usually represents either chronic hepatitis or nonalcoholic fatty liver disease.

How do we know if isolated ALT and/or AST elevations on screening blood profiles are due to strenuous exercise with muscle trauma?

We don't.

Which is why one of the most important bits of advice you can give your client is to MAKE SURE he does not have his paramedical within 7 days of intensive exercise and also that he abstains from any rigorous exercise within 24 hours of that exam.

If this advice is not adhered to – especially if your client competes in sporting events or is disposed to strenuous "workouts" – it could potentially result in ALT and/or AST elevations which the underwriter will have no choice but to either rate or postpone!

What is nonalcoholic fatty liver disease (NAFLD)?

It is the most common liver disorder in North America and the leading cause of elevated unsuspected liver tests on screening blood profiles in clinical medicine and insurance underwriting.

How do we know when elevated liver tests are due to this condition?

We cannot know for certain unless further clinical tests are done.

The most predictive scenario would be when:

- Only ALT is elevated, or, if AST is also elevated, the ratio favors ALT.
- The proposed insured is obese and has at least one or more of the five criteria for the so-called metabolic syndrome. (See Chapter 12.)

Is nonalcoholic fatty liver disease a significant risk?

This depends on which type of fatty liver is present:

- Simple steatosis – which is harmless so long as it remains as it is and does not progress.
- Steatohepatitis – which can, but usually doesn't, go on to cirrhosis and liver cancer.

Steatohepatitis in this context is usually referred to by the acronym NASH (nonalcoholic steatohepatitis) to distinguish it from alcoholic steatohepatitis, a far more serious disorder.

Other impairments which can be due to elevated ALT and AST more than rarely:

- Chronic hepatitis B
- Chronic hepatitis C
- Hemochromatosis, primarily in persons of Northern European, British, Scottish or Irish extraction

Many insurers will require the hepatitis C test when ALT is elevated. Some will do this for elevations of either ALT or AST. They may also order hepatitis B tests as well.

What is GGT?

It is an enzyme found in the liver as well as in a number of other organs.

Its full name is gamma-glutamyltransferase and, while the correct acronym is GGT, we also see GGTP used as well.

What can cause an elevation of GGT?

To answer this question accurately, we need to know that there are three distinctive mechanisms which can lead to an elevated GGT:

- Organ damage – almost always in the liver or bile ducts connected to the liver (even though GGT is found in other organs as well).

- Enzyme induction – which occurs in the liver but is not a cause of liver damage.
- Oxidative damage to the body – which is caused by imbalance between exposure to oxidants (toxic substances) and one's inventory of anti-oxidants (which neutralize oxidants and may prevent them from causing damage).

ORGAN DAMAGE: Any type of damage to the liver cells or the ducts between the liver and the organs in the "biliary tree" (consisting of, in addition to the liver, the pancreas and gallbladder) – can elevate GGT. This includes damage caused by certain medications, herbs and other compounds.

ENZYME INDUCTION: When exposed to an enzyme-inducing substance, one of the liver's responses is to release excess quantities of GGT. The main culprits here are alcohol and a few specific medications.

OXIDATIVE DAMAGE: GGT is a subtle clue to organ damage that may precede or accompany the onset of hypertension, diabetes and coronary artery disease. This role for GGT has only become widely known in recent years and it may complicate our assessment of GGT elevations.

What questions must the underwriter deal with, when confronted with a GGT elevation, in trying to decide its significance?

Is it an isolated GGT elevation? Which other tests are also abnormal?

If other tests are also elevated, additional possible causes need to be considered.

For example, elevations of GGT and HDL-C or AST suggest possible heavy drinking, whereas when GGT and alkaline phosphatase are both above normal our attention is focused on the bile ducts.

What are the main factors considered when the GGT elevation is

isolated (all other tests are normal)?

- How high is the GGT elevation?
- Does the proposed insured have a history of elevated GGT, abnormal liver tests or any type of liver or bile duct disease?
- Does he have any history related directly or indirectly to consuming excess alcohol or has he been diagnosed with alcohol abuse or dependency (alcoholism)?
- Has he ever had alcohol-related driving convictions?
- Does he currently take anticonvulsant* drugs? If so, are they ones which frequently elevate GGT through enzyme induction?
- Does he use over-the-counter remedies such as herbs or other digestibles? The herb kava (also called "kava kava") is used for anxiety and has been shown to cause isolated GGT elevations in healthy users with no evidence of liver damage.
- Does the insured have hypertension, diabetes or coronary disease?
- Does he have risk factors associated with developing these disorders in the future?
- Have any alcohol marker tests been done and, if so, what were the results?

* These drugs are officially anticonvulsants (also called antiseizure medications) and used for seizure disorders. However, some of them are used more often for other disorders, especially psychiatric conditions. The number of conditions for which some anticonvulsants are used continues to increase every year.

Only after he assesses all of these considerations can the underwriter have a clear idea of how to best assess the risk of an isolated GGT elevation.

What if all of these factors check out as negative and the underwriter is left with just the GGT elevation?

Then, he will either take action based on the degree of elevation or order a recheck. In my opinion, rechecking GGT is a dubious practice because 80% of rechecks will also be elevated…and even if the repeat GGT is normal, we don't really know much more than we did before the case was held up for a new blood specimen!

The same alternatives apply to isolated elevations of most blood profile screening tests:

- You accept some level of abnormality (either an elevation or, for some tests, a "below normal" reading as well)
- You rate some further increment of abnormality
- You postpone those which are still more abnormal pending clinical assessment

Why do we get more pushback from physicians on GGT than on any other screening test?

Because of how clinical doctors regard GGT:

- Most doctors know a lot less about GGT than most underwriters do.
- What they read in their lab test handbooks is that GGT has only one contribution to make in practicing medicine: an inexpensive way of determining if an alkaline phosphatase elevation is due to a bone (GGT normal) or bile duct (GGT elevated) disorder.
- GGT is not included in many of the clinical blood profiles, so doctors encounter it less often than we do.
- They know GGT is associated with heavy drinking but they usually don't investigate this based only on isolated GGT elevation when there is nothing else to suggest that alcohol is being abused or that their patient's drinking habits are causing them any problems.
- They know nothing of underwriting and how our perspective on GGT is, by necessity, far different from theirs.

What do you tell doctors when you deal with them in this context?

I have handled hundreds of these situations and have yet to fail to put one "to rest."

The key is the difference between underwriting and medicine. For us, the bottom line is this: given a thousand people with an isolated GGT elevation (that cannot be explained by a harmless mechanism like enzyme induction) and another thousand who do not have elevated GGT, we know beyond any question that the mortality – all other things being equal – must be worse in the first group.

Why?

- Because a significant number of them will be heavy drinkers – more so than in those with normal GGT.
- Because many will be experiencing silent oxidative damage, putting them at increased risk for major impairments (hypertension, type 2 diabetes and coronary disease) – more so than in those with normal GGT.
- Because some of them will have undiagnosed liver disease – more so than those with normal GGT.

Therefore, the sum of these factors must inevitably culminate in higher mortality for the group with elevated GGT as compared to the group with normal GGT.

Do insurance medical directors agree with you on this assessment?

I hope so…because I'm 100% correct!

Nevertheless, there will always be some who have not adequately investigated this subject, perhaps because their prior clinical perspectives are ingrained in their thinking.

As French physiologist Claude Bernard once said:

> *"It is what we think we already know that often prevents us from learning."*

CHAPTER 8

———•———•———•———•———

Preferred Risk Underwriting

What is meant by "preferred risk"?

Most life insurers offer coverage on some or all products wherein the proposed insured may qualify by a finite set of criteria for premium rates lower than those charged for "standard" risks. These premium rates have been designated as "preferred" and we will use the word "preferred" hereafter as a synonym for "preferred risk."

When did most companies begin offering preferred coverage?

Roughly 15% began writing it prior to 1990. Then its use escalated steeply in the mid-1990s, and by the turn of the millennium 70% were making preferred coverage available on some basis.

Do most carriers offer preferred rates on all of their fully underwritten life products?

Yes. Roughly 60% do so.

Do some offer more than one preferred risk class?

Actually, the vast majority have at least two non-tobacco preferred classes, and three out of four also offer what is commonly referred to as "smoker preferred."

One in four writes four or more and there are a few who somehow manage to conjure up enough distinctions to offer as many as six!

This said, most chief underwriters would likely agree that there are three core preferred classes: preferred, super preferred and smoker preferred.

What has been the recent trend as far as number of preferred classes offered?

According to a comprehensive survey, four out of ten insurers have changed that number and nearly all of these have added at least one new class.

Why?

No doubt competitive pressure is a driver here, but one must also consider that studies over the last 15 years have, in the main, supported the validity of the preferred concept and this has encouraged many companies to venture forward with new innovations.

What are the dominant factors used to develop and support criteria for defining "preferred" in its various iterations?

Dominant Preferred Risk Criteria in Life Underwriting

- Age
- Tobacco/nicotine use status
- Weight
- Blood pressure
- Cholesterol
- High density lipoprotein cholesterol (HDL-C)
- The ratio of cholesterol to HDL-C
- Family history
- Driving record
- Aviation
- Avocations
- History of substance abuse
- Citizenship status
- GGT

Do most insurers apply the same preferred criteria at all ages?

The majority do…but the pace at which this is changing continues to accelerate (as it should).

Realistically, there are three distinct age groupings where preferred criteria should differ significantly:

- 18 to 35 or 40
- 35 or 40 to 65 or 70
- 65 or 70 and older

What are the main factors used in defining preferred classes?

Primary Drivers in Setting Preferred Risk Criteria

- Advice from reinsurers
- Internal and external (published) mortality studies
- Judgment of underwriting management
- Protective value (cost-benefit) studies
- Advice from medical directors, actuaries and outside consultants
- Discussions at both formal industry meetings and study groups
- Dart boards (Judging from some of what's out there!)

For the record, this formidable list will continue to grow for two reasons:

1. New (and mostly better) options are emerging.
2. Pressure will be exerted from various elements to "stick with what works."

What are the youngest and oldest ages at which most insurers offer preferred?

On the youthful side, age 18 is most widely used; then, age 20, and a smattering younger or older.

On the elderly side, upwards of 40% appear to write preferred on some basis over age 80 and there is a small minority who quit under age 70.

There is reason to suspect that some carriers may pull back on preferred offerings over age 70, and especially over age 80, in the years ahead.

How is weight configured in preferred?

Build (weight in relation to height) is still the mainstay despite its inferiority to body mass index (BMI).

With minimal-impact caveats, it will be a great day for all when:

- BMI replaces build.
- Either is further modified by waist and/or waist-to-hip circumference.

Do insurers using BMI set lower limits below which preferred is denied?

Indeed they do (as they should), while properly granting some "wiggle room" where the proposed insured has been rather thin lifelong and in the absence of an adverse medical reason.

What are the prevalent preferred thresholds for blood pressure?

As you would expect, they loosen up with age and, like most criteria, are tighter for super-preferred than for the first level of preferred.

Which aspects of older-age preferred risk BP underwriting need further scrutiny by insurers?

1. Being too liberal with systolic elevations from the low 140s up to 160.
2. Just the opposite with diastolic readings in the 90s.

3. Waking up to the importance of pulse pressure* as a modifying factor by age 70; maybe even younger.

* Pulse pressure (PP) is the number you get by subtracting the diastolic reading from its systolic counterpart. Therefore, if your BP is 140/90, your pulse pressure is normal at 50. When PP is 70 or higher, it is generally held to be too high and usually reflects stiffening of the arteries.

Do any companies set BP minimums, below which they deny preferred?

Not many, and those that do use minimums only for their best class of preferred. This is another matter which needs further consideration where elderly applicants are concerned.

Do most insurers allow applicants with well-controlled hypertension to get preferred coverage?

Yes, and they should, unless:

- Other cardiovascular risk factors are present.
- The proposed insured does not take the blood pressure medication as prescribed.

Failure to take medication as prescribed is called either "nonadherence" or "noncompliance." The fact that it leaves the high blood pressure uncontrolled is just one of its adverse implications for insurability.

Where is the emphasis placed on blood lipids in preferred risk?

On the total cholesterol/HDL-cholesterol ratio, even though most carriers also set upper limits for both readings individually.

For best preferred class, we are not (with good reason) too flexible, and maximum ratios hover in the 4.5 to 5.5 range. This eases up to

6.5 or a bit higher in the other preferred classes.

If the ratio matters most, why be concerned about total cholesterol and HDL-C readings individually?

Because ratios can be notoriously misleading when one or both ratio components are at one end or the other of the bell curve, so to speak.

For example, consider two male applicants with an identical TC:HDL-C ratio of 3. As ratios go, 3 is "top class preferred" by everyone's reckoning.

The first fellow has a TC of 180 and an HDL-C of 60. Both are "thumbs up" and result in this favorable ratio. The other man, however, has readings of 300 and 100 respectively and while they also happen to net out to a ratio of 3, TC of 300 is way too high and HDL-C of 100 may be due to sinister unfavorable causes such as alcohol abuse.

Are triglycerides factored into preferred risk?

Yes, in nearly all companies...as they should be, considering that we now know that they are at least as significant as total cholesterol.

Does it matter if the triglycerides reading is measured in a fasting state?

A minority of companies only use fasting levels for preferred.

This approach, however, is questionable at best because we now know that readings done after eating are every bit as significant to risk as those taken in a fasting state.

Do insurers set minimum levels for any lipid readings in a preferred context?

Yes.

In HDL-C, very low levels in the range of 35 or less in a male and 40 or lower in a female are associated with an increased risk of circulatory disease. This is largely but not entirely accounted for by using the TC-to-HDL-C ratio.

With cholesterol, however, the scenario changes with very low readings. Here the concern focuses mainly over age 60 and is often accompanied by physical frailty in the elderly.

Do all insurers set cholesterol minimums for preferred?

No – but they should!

What is considered "too low" in this context?

Some medical studies make a case for readings as "high" as 160 being unfavorable while others would set the minimum lower. My threshold is 140 and most insurers who use minimums set them even lower.

Do any factors influence the impact of low readings?

Yes. There are 3 that should:

1. If the proposed insured is currently on treatment for high cholesterol, in which case at least borderline low readings are not considered unfavorable.
2. If readings have been progressively declining in the absence of cholesterol-lowering medication, this is far more worrisome in the presence of a very low level.
3. Other risk factors for general debility or frailty act synergistically with low cholesterol to worsen the risk. Some of these are:

   - Underweight and/or recent unintentional weight loss
   - Very low triglycerides and/or HDL-C
   - Low readings on certain other lab tests, such as serum (blood) albumin, triglycerides, etc.
   - Long history of heavy cigarette smoking

Do most insurers allow individuals on treatment for cholesterol or other lipid abnormalities to qualify for preferred on some basis?

Yes, just as they do with treated and well-controlled blood pressure.

Can a well-controlled diabetic qualify for preferred?

In 10% or so of companies, you will find guidelines accommodating this. However, I take diabetes and even prediabetic states very seriously and so I don't think this is appropriate. It sends the wrong message.

What other medical risk considerations have worked their way into preferred criteria in recent years?

- Specific criteria for cognitive functioning and physical frailty in the elderly, a trend that is increasing rapidly and should become universal.
- The blood test glycosylated hemoglobin (HbA1-c), which is the marker we use for assessing blood sugar control in diabetics. In the preferred context, we are starting to use it whether or not diabetes is present because it is a solid marker for mortality on this basis as well.
- Additional blood tests including the exemplary heart-related marker NT-proBNP, creatinine (more so, ideally, cystatin C), and the liver enzymes GGT, ALT and AST.
- We should realistically add the uric acid blood test as well as a mathematically derived marker known as estimated glomerular filtration rate (eGFR; a test for decline in kidney function).

How do insurers approach tobacco/nicotine use for preferred?

Except for "smoker preferred," nearly all preferred products require abstinence from at least cigarette smoking for a stated interval.

What is the most frequent stipulation in this context?

The vast majority consider "use of tobacco or nicotine in any form" as disqualifying for preferred (again, with the exception of "smoker preferred" rates).

Where companies do not lump all tobacco and nicotine use together in this fashion, what are the most common elements allowed for preferred?

- Smokeless tobacco, which some have never excluded from preferred.
- One or more criteria permitting a specified level of cigar use.

How long must a smoker/nicotine user have quit in order to qualify for non-smoker preferred?

It used to be almost universally 12 months, but we are seeing a trend toward going out 24 to 36 months.

To qualify for best preferred class, many companies now insist on 60 months tobacco- and nicotine-free.

What is the ideal approach in this regard?

In my opinion:

1. Making cigarette smokers wait at least 3 years; less time for all other tobacco users.
2. Using the "pack-year" concept to set a total consumption threshold beyond which the individual can no longer qualify for "non-user" status on any basis.

Do most insurers include some elements of family history in their preferred criteria?

Yes – nearly all have a circulatory disease criterion covering heart attacks and strokes, focused solely on first degree relatives (natural parents and siblings).

Which other types of family history are used by the majority?

- Cancer
- Diabetes

Beyond this, a few use dementia and, uncommonly, a few others.

Does family history relate to first degree relatives only?

I haven't seen a life company use grandparents, aunts, uncles, etc.

Which makes sense because this would be a stretch for most common diseases.

Besides, getting this approved by regulators would be nearly impossible and the quality of the histories we would get on second degree relatives wouldn't be worth much.

Are preferred family histories limited to deaths only or do they also include nonfatal events?

The last data I saw – and it is from 2008 – shows that the majority continue to benchmark death from MI, stroke, cancer, etc., in lieu of events. This approach defies common sense, considering that whether one's parent or sib dies or survives these problems misses the whole purpose of asking about family history in the first place!

Dying vs. surviving is a random consideration due to factors wholly unrelated to the risk of family members developing the condition.

Do the threshold ages at which deaths or events are counted differ widely between companies?

They do, ranging from 70 or under on one end of the spectrum to 55 or younger on the other. They may also be the same for both genders, which does not make a lot of sense where heart attacks and strokes are concerned.

Why?

Because women are conferred hormone-induced advantages which delay the onset of coronary disease as well as strokes from their most common cause.

It is reasonable to argue that a heart attack in a 70-year-old mother equates – in terms of relative risk to the proposed insured – to that of an MI in a 65-…if not 60-…year-old father!

For this reason, I believe there should be at least a 5-year offset between males (younger age threshold) and females.

Are applicants' driving records factored into preferred risk practices?

Yes, for impaired driving as well as for grossly unfavorable driving records which do not include convictions for being drunk or drugged behind the wheel.

How long does a proposed insured typically have to wait to qualify for preferred following an impaired driving conviction?

Five years is most common for preferred on some basis.

For best preferred risk class, waiting 6 to 10 years is typical. Some insurers go so for as permanently disqualifying applicants from best preferred rates for this reason.

What kinds of violations other than impaired driving are considered in terms of overall driving record?

- Suspended or revoked license
- Reckless driving
- Large number of moving violations, either overall or within a stated time interval

Not accidents?

To the best of my knowledge, accidents are not used as a routine criteria. But remember, in most jurisdictions if one has an accident and is clearly at fault, a citation for some moving violation (or worse) is often issued.

How do insurers handle alcohol and drug abuse in terms of when one may qualify for preferred?

Practices vary considerably, from less than 5 years (especially for preferred on any basis) to 10 years or longer. In addition, a substantial number permanently disqualify these risks from best class preferred.

This approach applies to illicit drug abuse or dependency as well.

How does being an aviator relate to preferred eligibility?

Some companies will not issue preferred on any basis, others will do so only with an exclusion rider and the largest subset will allow some types of flying at least to qualify even without a rider. As one might expect, commercial, regularly scheduled flying is most apt to be allowed into preferred classes.

Are hazardous avocations and occupations managed in the same manner?

Actually, practices here differ widely, from denial of preferred to issuing on this basis even if the avocation or occupation requires a flat extra premium.

Do most insurers report favorable mortality results on preferred business?

The majority say it has been more or less as expected. However, in a recent survey over 30% said mortality turned out to be "better than expected" whereas only a few reported unfavorable outcomes.

One would have to conclude that these largely favorable findings "cement" the preferred concept and, sooner or later, will lead to its embrace in most major global life markets.

CHAPTER 9

———•———•———•———•———

Teleunderwriting

What is teleunderwriting?

Teleunderwriting means taking the applicant's risk history over the telephone, instead of non-medically (by the producer) or in conjunction with a paramedical or M.D. exam.

What are the two components of the teleinterview?

1. The baseline interview, which asks essentially the same questions currently used in conventional history-taking.
2. "Drilldown questioning," which is done whenever the applicant answers YES to a question on the baseline interview. The teleinterviewer has a specific list of questions for this purpose.

Drilldown questions often differ greatly depending upon the matter under scrutiny. For example, if it is diabetes, some questions will focus specifically on issues related to this impairment, such as vision, kidney and nerve problems.

What makes teleinterviews superior to conventional history-taking?

The quantity and quality of information gathered on the drilldown questioning – as compared to what is typically disclosed in conventional history-taking – when we ask applicants to elaborate on YES answers to baseline application questions.

Although producers, paramedical technicians and examining physicians are supposed to expand upon YES answers thoroughly, this seldom happens to the extent we would like. With drilldown questioning, on the other hand, all of the necessary questions are asked and answered.

When did teleunderwriting begin?

In the late 1980's, as an experiment by a handful of proactive insurers.

What were the first attempts called?

Personal history interviews (PHIs), in which only baseline history-taking was done with little if any drilldown questioning.

Some companies still do PHIs, but they have largely been replaced by true teleunderwriting.

How widely used is teleunderwriting today?

The latest survey (2007) shows that 3 out of 4 life carriers make routine use of teleinterviews with drilldown questioning on some or all of their business.

Why don't the remaining 25% of insurers make use of teleunderwriting at this time?

The 2007 survey showed that over 70% of these companies had not yet even experimented with teleinterviews. They need to understand that they are now at a major competitive disadvantage...and start catching up!

Roughly 1 in 6 of the companies that are not doing teleinterviews said they had considered adopting this process but decided against it. It's hard for me to conceive of any scenario involving fully underwritten business where teleunderwriting would not be superior to the ways of the past. Therefore, in my view at least, they are making an even bigger mistake than the 70% who have yet to assess this process!

Why not do teleunderwriting on all cases?

We should!

Unfortunately, there are still insurers who limit teleinterviewing to certain products, face amounts and/or applicant ages.

At older ages, for example, some believe that the teleinterview with drilldown questioning is not necessary because they are likely to require an APS on the majority of cases.

They're wrong, because teleinterviews inevitably contribute significant risk information they would not otherwise get…and sometimes this information will allow them to forego the APS or modify how they interpret what is reported on the APS.

Why not use a website-based approach, asking the application questions and then any drilldown questions needed, instead of the teleinterview?

Some companies do.

Hopefully, for their sake, they also price adequately for the drawbacks inherent in this approach!

What are those drawbacks?

- Computer fatigue – which means that if the application process drags on due to multiple risk history factors requiring expanded (drilldown) questioning, many persons will simply stop and terminate the whole process. The net result is the loss of potentially

insurable business.
- Misrepresentation – answering the questions, and especially the drilldown component, on-line affords the applicant a golden opportunity to get advice and counsel from others who may be present. As a rule, the longer the applicant has to consider his response, the greater the probability of intentional nondisclosure, as well as untruthful replies.

Why can't applicants be as non-disclosing and untruthful on teleinterviews as they can with on-line history-taking?

Oh, they can…in theory…if they are well-prepared, know or anticipate what is going to be asked and resolve to lie either indirectly (not disclosing) or directly (giving untruthful answers).

However, as best as we can determine – after matching up drilldown answers with APS content – the incidence of this is far lower than with either traditional or on-line history-taking.

What factors may account for this advantage to teleinterviews?

- They are dealing with a pleasant (and usually female) voice, not a machine. It is more difficult for most people to lie in this setting.
- Long pauses, as well as changed, muddled and incomplete responses, are noted by the teleinterviewer – they are trained to do this – and then reported back to the underwriter. When this happens, the odds of an APS being ordered go way up!
- Teleinterviewers can ask for clarification; machines cannot.

I recommend to my clients that they specifically stipulate that the producer must not be present and always ask about this at the start of the interview. If the producer is present, I advise them to terminate the interview and ask the applicant when it would be convenient to reschedule the call when he will be alone.

I hope you don't take offense at this last point.

Like persons in any line of work, 99%+ of producers are honest, forthright individuals who would never stoop to encouraging their clients to be non-disclosing, let alone to give overtly untruthful answers.

Nevertheless, that tiny rogue minority can have a substantially adverse impact on the mortality or morbidity of the whole block of business.

Therefore, since there is no compelling reason why the producer should be present during the teleinterview, I prefer to proactively stipulate that the teleinterview be done when the producer is not present.

Are teleinterviews recorded?

Yes, in virtually every case.

Why?

To protect all parties in the event there is a dispute as to what was said.

I've heard scattered anecdotal reports that these records have had a significant impact in situations where insurers need to rescind or reform an in-force, as well is in contested claims. Common sense says that this should be the case, as we have the actual voice of the insured answering the questions.

Where are teleinterviews done?

Roughly 60% of insurers outsource all of their teleinterviews to firms that specialize in doing them, 25% do all teleinterviews in-house with their own employes and the remaining 15% do both (outsourcing some; doing the rest at the home office).

Why is outsourcing so prevalent?

- The start-up costs of a teleunderwriting program are far lower and the time to commencement much faster using outsourced callers.

- In many parts of the country, it is difficult to hire new teleinterviewers with prior experience.
- Insurers can readily monitor the caliber of outsourced calls.
- Outsourced interviews, for the most part, have proven to be very adequately done.

Are most of the teleinterviewers experienced in underwriting?

Less than 10% in the latest survey and the good money says the percentage is far lower now, for several reasons:

- We don't have enough trained underwriters as it is!
- In most situations, underwriters would take a pay cut if they did teleinterviewing instead.
- It's highly unlikely that most underwriters, by their nature, would find interviewing applicants all day long as rewarding as what they do.

What is the background of most teleinterviewers?

Probably 15-20% have prior new business department experience, typically as an underwriter assistant or in a clerical function.

There is also a growing number of nurses in teleinterviewing, especially those who want to get away from clinical nursing for personal reasons and, in many cases, these individuals work from home much like telecommuting underwriters.

The remaining component, which likely accounts for 50% or more, is made up of individuals with no relevant experience where underwriting or insurance is concerned. However, many have worked in call centers and the rest are trained in call-center skills before they are turned loose to do teleinterviews.

Are all teleinterviews scripted?

Yes…although there are a few who allow underwriters or nurses working as teleinterviewers to improvise.

I think every teleinterview should be scripted. However, I don't think that teleinterviewers should be restricted to asking only scripted questions because all too often the answers given by applicants are incomplete and another question or two can get at what is really needed.

In Great Britain, it is commonplace for skilled teleinterviewers to go off-script whenever they see the need for more information. I'm told by UK chief underwriters that this works magnificently.

My prediction is that we will embrace this approach in North America, provided outsourced providers can raise the skill levels of their teleinterviewers to get the job done.

How long is the average teleinterview?

Insurers and service providers have cited mean interview times for life business in the range of 10-14 minutes. To a great degree, the duration of the interview depends on the length of the baseline interview (which is determined by the number of the application's risk questions) and the number of YES answers requiring drilldown questioning.

Interviews always take longer, on average, for full-underwritten DI and long term care applications. The average duration varies widely in health insurance, but most are at least as long as life teleinterviews.

For the record, the longest teleinterview I've ever heard of took 3 hours. It was done in England on an application for both life and DI (they call it "income protection"), and took two interviews, each lasting 90 minutes or so, to be completed. They told me the life policy was issued…but the DI was declined!

How do we get the interviews "signed" by the proposed insureds?

As I write this, the majority are probably still being signed on delivery. However, use of both electronic and voice signatures is growing rapidly. In the 2007 survey, 25% were using electronic and 12% voice.

Hopefully, voice signatures will come to dominate here because they are the most convenient and, I would wager, most reliable (considering how sophisticated the science of voice analysis is now).

What factors have caused most insurers to move on from traditional risk-history taking to teleinterviewing?

I can think of 7 that have motivated them:

- Shortened application-to-issue cycle time
- Reduced business acquisition costs
- Increased quantity and quality of risk information, so that underwriters can make better decisions
- Reduced dependence on medical records
- Making it easier for customers to do business with the company
- Helping producers increase their productivity by lessening the amount of time they must spend on "home office matters"
- Keeping pace with competitors who have already embraced tele-underwriting and are enjoying significant competitive advantages

Which of these is probably the most important where insurers are concerned?

Reducing cycle time, as reflected in this observation by Bob Kerzner, President of LIMRA and CEO of recently merged LIMRA and LOMA, cited in the November 5, 2007, issue of *The National Underwriter*:

> *"Among the most important outcomes, Kerzner predicted, within the next 5 to 10 years would be a dramatic shortening of the lead time required for processing a life insurance policy."*

Is cycle time important to producers?

> *"Agents invest time and use skill to bring the customers to the point of filling out the application...then time passes – often lots of it – often six weeks or more before the application is approved...By reducing the approval process by just a couple of weeks, we could cut the default figures* [lost sales] *in half."*

> Ron Verzone
> United Underwriters Inc; Exeter, NH
> "Remember the Customer"
> *Best's Review*
> October 2003

Ron's comments are buttressed by these findings:

In his article "What Producers Want," *Best's Review* Senior Editor Ron Panko reported that cycle time ranked #2 in terms of factors considered by producers when choosing which carriers to do business with. [*Best's Review*; March 2004]

That same year, a paper for insurers titled "Insights into Strengthening Producer Relationships" by Denise Marvel of LIMRA also cited prompt issuance of policies as ranking #2 in importance to producers...and #1 as an "area that needs improvement."

What are the prevailing average cycle times in the industry?

An informal survey conducted by a member of one of my study groups found that this ranged from 18 to 30 days, with the average among the 7 major carriers being just under 23 days.

23 days!

If there was ever an argument for teleunderwriting, this number makes that argument!

In that same survey, non-medicals were faster, averaging around 16 days, whereas paramedicals were in the range of 27 days. No data were specifically cited for the dwindling portion of M.D.-examined business (but you can bet it is longer than paramedical time!).

Have insurers reported significant improvements in cycle time from teleunderwriting?

In my study groups, most teleunderwriting-driven companies say teleunderwriting has had a significantly favorable impact on cycle time.

Those not enjoying this outcome invariably have correctable problems with one or more facets of how they teleunderwrite. Companies I've worked with as a consultant have readily made changes which lead to lowering cycle time.

What is the #1 factor impacting cycle time?

If the insurer is paper-based, then this is always the leading reason for lousy cycle time.

In most others, it is lag time in getting the slowest (widely used) requirement we have: the APS.

How can insurers deal with APS slowness?

- Find a way to speed up the process
- Order less of them

Most try to do both.

How does teleunderwriting impact APS ordering?

It provides sufficient medical history information to make final underwriting decisions on cases where underwriters would have ordered an APS (or two, or…!) in the past.

Has teleunderwriting accomplished this mission?

Absolutely!

In the 2007 survey, over 75% of companies said APS ordering has been reduced due to teleinterviews.

As I reported in *Best's Review* in my August 2004 essay "Making Producers Happy," one "top ten" life company ordered an APS on 40% of their business prior to teleunderwriting and cut that back to just 15% after teleunderwriting was embraced for a couple of years. Right now, there are companies getting ridiculously excessive numbers of medical records because they have either not begun teleunderwriting or are doing something wrong in how they use the process.

How does the APS stack up compared to the teleinterview?

Impact of the APS vs. the Teleinterview (where it matters most)		
	APS	**Teleinterview**
Acquisition time	12-18+ days	1-3 days
Cost	$60+ and rising	$15-25
Producer impact	Impatience	Joy
Customer reaction	Irritation	Satisfaction

Can't something be done to speed up the APS?

Believe me, we've tried everything we can think of!

Firms specializing in this function have substantially lowered acquisition times from those we suffered under when insurers pursued medical records directly from doctors and hospitals on their own.

Is there hope that with the advent of electronic medical records this

will change?

Eventually – years from now – sure.

However, only a small minority of physicians have electronic medical record-keeping in use (in one study, 5% had full access and only 15% overall had any type of electronic records), and there are formidable obstacles to overcome before the situation changes dramatically.

What we have now, for the most part, are electronic medical records which can be edited by patients. No need to explain why these records are useless in underwriting!

Can all cases be underwritten with a teleinterview in lieu of an APS?

No – not invasive cancers, heart attacks, serious chronic diseases, etc.

We will always need medical records on such impairments as well as complicated multifactorial medical histories on most – but not all – elderly applicants.

Are there impairments which used to cause underwriters to routinely order an APS but can now be underwritten without medical records by virtue of teleunderwriting?

Hundreds of them, including many of the most common histories we encounter:

- Headaches
- Chest pain
- Rectal bleeding
- Palpitations
- Fainting
- Asthma
- Colitis
- Acid reflux
- Arthritis

- Anxiety and even depression

Does this mean we never need to get an APS on these impairments?

No.

But we can triage them based on what is disclosed on the drilldown and avoid getting an APS on at least 50% of them. With some of these common medical problems, the number where an APS is no longer needed may be 80% or more.

What is the main determining factor as to whether or not we succeed here?

> *"Any of you who have gone through a teleunderwriting or e-app process know that can be a real paradigm shift, to get underwriters to quit ordering APS's on some things they have traditionally ordered APS's on."*

> Jennifer Richards
> Principal Financial
> AHOU* Annual Meeting
> Proceedings; page 167

*AHOU is the Association of Home Office Underwriters, the national U.S. life underwriters' organization.

Do most underwriters embrace teleunderwriting?

Yes. They don't have any vested interest in seeing pending cases drag on needlessly when they could be making decisions faster!

While teleunderwriting has not been a traumatic adjustment for most of my peers, there have been some who simply could not get comfortable with letting go of APS ordering in situations where it was no longer necessary. Most of them had been doing things the traditional way for decades and hence were already approaching retirement age.

How do reinsurers regard teleunderwriting?

It has been a long "courtship," but most reinsurers are comfortable with teleunderwriting. In fact, some are giving "mortality credits" (lower prices) to their best clients who do make effective (and adequately audited) use of teleunderwriting.

No one can blame reinsurers for being skeptical early on. It was incumbent on insurers to show that they could change to teleunder-writing and continue to do high quality risk assessment. Now that they have, one senses that reinsurer pushback has given way to what one might call "attentive support."

Has their success with teleunderwriting led some companies to rethink their screening requirements?

I raised this very question in an informal survey of a group of major carriers and 78% of them said YES.

The name of the game, as ever, is making certain there is sufficient overall protective value. If a bountiful pay-off occurs because of tele-underwriting, and this leads to better mortality results, the insurer is likely, sooner or later, to parlay this into reducing business acquisition costs. This, in turn, often translates into what producers will regard as "liberalizations" in screening requirements.

Some will argue that this process takes too long, and sometimes they will be right (insurers, for the most part, tend to move cautiously because there is so much at stake here). Nevertheless, it is in their best interests to make prudent changes and, fortunately for all concerned, those changes usually translate to getting rid of the most unpalatable requirements (treadmills, chest x-rays, M.D. examinations, and so on)!

How do the insurance regulators feel about teleunderwriting?

I have no idea. That is, other than being told of relatively little pushback in those states where insurers have been asked to file drilldown questionnaires.

In the UK, the Association of British Insurers issued a lengthy manifesto which did more than "merely" endorse teleunderwriting. Their position, as I interpret it, mandates that insurers embrace the teleunderwriting process.

This, of course, makes sense because teleunderwriting allows the applicant – whose interests the ABI looks after – unprecedented opportunity for direct input to insurers regarding his risk history.

How do the "C" folks – as in CEO, COO, etc. – at insurers feel about teleunderwriting?

In a recent small survey, every chief underwriter said the same thing: "Top brass" is pleased the company went in this direction. You'd expect they would be, considering how lower costs and faster policy approvals are two of their goals!

What has been the reaction of producers to teleunderwriting?

Overall, favorable – given that there are (and probably always will be) some who find fault with just about everything we do!

In the aforementioned survey 1/3rd of companies said producers "love" teleunderwriting while the rest chose the term "tolerate" instead. Best of all: none resorted to "they hate it" (the third optional response)!

Once producers apprehend all the reasons they should love teleunderwriting, there is usually a pretty quick buy-in (see the table **Why Producers Should Love Teleunderwriting** on the following page).

Why Producers Should Love Teleunderwriting

- Selling – not taking risk histories – is the best use of a producer's time.

- A SLOW APS can lose a sale; a SLOW, UNNECESSARY APS can lose a sale UNNECESSARILY.

- Sometimes, taking a client's history can lead to embarrassing moments. One leader in brokerage underwriting said this to me: "I can't believe how many agents tell me they don't want to get into their clients' medical histories with them since they feel it is too personal."

- There can be major producer liability in this context. I was involved in a case of spouse coverage where the producer knew the family well, the husband was a longtime client with whom he golfed often, their wives socialized, they'd vacationed together and so on. The spouse had a history of repeated inpatient treatment for depression but the non-medical was, shall we say, "extraordinarily vague" about this point. Then, there was a claim and the insurer wound up taking legal action against the agent because they felt that, knowing what he must have known, he didn't do his job and they'd issued coverage to someone they would have declined…if he had.

- Payoffs from teleunderwriting protective value allow liberalizations on other requirements.

- Less APS ordering makes clients happy. This has always been the one aspect our customers have liked the least about underwriting.

- No more "incompletes"! Prior to teleunderwriting, companies had outrageously high levels of incomplete applications which had to go back to the producer. Incompletes are impossible with properly done teleunderwriting.

- Sooner or later, teleunderwriting reduces acquisition costs. This lessens the risk that cost control worries could "spill over" into producer compensation.

Is there any one issue related to teleunderwriting that producers raise?

Yes. I call it the "control myth."

This myth holds that teleunderwriting takes control of the client away from the agent, jeopardizing the producer/client relationship, and hence the sale.

What I don't understand is how this happens – that is, of course, if the nature of the producer's control is such that it is a detriment to the insurer!

Since the only difference here is that the risk history is taken over the phone, how does this compromise control? The producer still needs to get a strong feel for the medical history on a fact-finding basis or he won't know whether to apply for "super preferred" or expect a rated policy!

If the teleinterviewer does something to offend the client, that could have an adverse impact, true…but this risk already exists where paramedical technicians are concerned and it is far more likely to cause a ruckus when you take measurements and collect various bodily fluids.

The huge advantages to the producer from teleunderwriting trump (largely imaginary) "control" issues.

How should a producer prepare his client for a teleinterview?

- Tell him he will get a phone call from a person whose only job is to ask questions and record answers.
- This individual is a professional caller. She has no interest in his history other than faithfully recording what he says in answer to her scripted questions.
- Everything he says is recorded for his protection and held in the strictest confidence.
- Have him decide when it is best for the call to be done and

provide his phone number to you so you can share his chosen time and phone number with the insurer.

- Advise him that, if he takes medication, he should ideally have the pill bottles in hand when the call comes through, because the caller will ask for certain details (drug name, dosage, times taken per day).

- Remind him that the teleinterview has become routine in the industry in part because it allows him to provide more information about his history. By doing this, the client reduces the chances that medical records will be sought and has the opportunity to "state his case" for the record, so to speak.

Are any clients lousy candidates for teleinterviews?

Sure. Those...

- ...who have a belligerent personality could cause the interview to be stopped prematurely.

- ...with heavy accents may not be easily understood over the phone. Fortunately, many companies now provide for interviewing in one or more languages other than English.

- ...whom you know, by personal experience, may drive the teleinterviewer bonkers asking her a lot of questions she can't answer!

In these rare cases, you probably need to discuss the matter with your underwriter before proceeding.

Is there anything that could be infused into teleunderwriting to make it more effective for all?

Yes.

Health habit questions!

We know so much now from medical studies and other sources about how both the healthy and unhealthy practices people choose to embrace influence their mortality and morbidity risks.

As far back as 1980, Manufacturers Life's chief actuary, Robin Leckie, lectured to Canadian insurance doctors about "lifestyle underwriting" and why it should be done. I prefer "health habits" over "lifestyle," if only to avoid any misconceptions regarding matters such as sexual orientation (which, of course, has no place in underwriting).

What Robin wanted wasn't possible back then, but it is now, with teleunderwriting.

In the 2007 Requirement Survey, I asked respondents if any of them include these matters in routine underwriting.

15% said YES, while an additional 11% were considering this.

What are the future prospects?

It is crystal clear that both health habits and risk-taking behaviors have a legitimate place in underwriting. Finally, with teleunderwriting, we have what we need to get this done. Fact is, insurers in the United Kingdom are doing some of this right now.

In other words, YES, it is destined to happen. When it does, it will confer a major advantage on insurance seekers who practice desirable health habits and shun risk-taking behaviors.

What is an "underwriting engine"?

It is a technology asset designed to do some degree of assessment of risk electronically, without the underwriter being directly involved. In other words, automated underwriting.

Who makes these engines?

Software firms as well as several reinsurers.

Are companies using them?

Not many in North America yet. However, they're used extensively in Britain and elsewhere. No doubt part of the reason for their appeal outside North America are the comparatively smaller face amounts and greater reliance on products with robust pricing margins found in other markets.

Is teleunderwriting involved in the process?

Sometimes but not always.

What are the arguments for using them?

> *"Business rule and decisioning technologies are key components of exception-based underwriting and allow the insurer to put their business rules and processes into a tool that can automate the process... This serves to reduce underwriting workload, since they are concentrating on exceptions, and improve the speed of underwriting."*
>
> Kimberly Harris
> Gartner Group
> *LOMA Resource*
> November 2004

> *"Companies have realized their new business pipelines are inefficient and that they need to cut costs, move to e-business, improve their service to producers (instant acceptances and simpler new business workflows) and generate better management information."*
>
> Susie Cour-Palais and Peter Maynard
> SelectX, UK
> *On The Risk*
> 22, 2 (2006):22

When is their use most appropriate?

In what we call "jet underwriting" (automated approval of smaller cases, mainly at younger ages, without review by an underwriter).

The number of jet-eligible cases for any insurer depends on a number of considerations including markets served, average face amount, etc. Overall, most carriers – that is, other than those heavily into the older-age and impaired-risk markets – could use jet underwriting on 15% to 40% of their new business.

The old narrow ranges for "jet underwriting" can be safely broadened in many companies with the use of well-designed underwriting engines. However, it is beyond fanciful to believe, as some engine manufacturers suggest, that 70% or more of fully underwritten applications can be appraised on this basis.

What about using engines on more complicated cases?

This is where we have strong differences of opinion on their potential contribution.

The fact that they appear to work well in Europe must not be construed as evidence that they can play the same proportional role on this side of "the pond."

The differences between our markets are just too great, in many key domains, for this stipulation to be valid.

Engine-driven underwriting is "by the book" underwriting. One would think most producers would be less than enamored of wider proliferation of this phenomenon!

Here is what two very talented gentlemen – a chief underwriter and his medical director – have to say on this subject:

"The art form of underwriting, when properly used,

*must consider the variables and all aspects of the
case before reaching the best decision on the risk to
be accepted. Sometimes, when going 'by the book' is
simply not the best approach, the art of underwriting
can be implemented with the intention of making
every rating as accurate as possible."*

> Everett Kunzelman and Clifford Hale, MD
> Jackson National Life
> *National Underwriter*
> November 12, 2007; page 30

What % of US and Canadian life business is destined to be "underwritten" by machines, based on their current capabilities?

As I say, there are some outlandish statements being circulated in this regard.

For example, one energized engine advocate working for a firm in this field wrote me an e-mail in response to an essay I'd done for *Best's Review*. In it, he fantasized about doing 70% to 90% of a typical insurer's new business in this manner.

This is patently impossible. Nevertheless, one cannot rule out senior management in some companies being lured into believing that they can enjoy alleged cost savings without paying a far greater price sliced off their bottom line.

No two cases are ever identical. Therefore, when machine-driven underwriting starts encroaching into non-jet eligible business, sacrifice of the art of underwriting will be felt, big time, by all parties to the transaction.

I don't imagine producers will get a warm and fuzzy feeling knowing that important considerations may have been left out because the machine cannot distinguish (let alone evaluate) them in context with the whole risk.

Who could be the biggest losers if engines are used more extensively than they should be?

The proposed insured.

Why?

Because the most equitable underwriting outcomes are realized when the art of underwriting is brought to bear. When this is sacrificed in favor of a formulaic approach, companies that have over-deployed underwriting engines could find themselves at a competitive disadvantage in terms of attracting the best business.

Frankly, I worry that lack of adequate senior management understanding of what underwriting (really) is all about could fuel overdependence on these engines. I say this because of a profoundly false presumption in some quarters that what we underwriters do can be reduced to sets of rules. Equally so that machines can somehow be programmed to recognize and then deal with most risk appraisal scenarios where human judgment should be brought to bear.

This isn't auto insurance, folks – it is insurance covering marvelously complex organisms called *Homo sapiens*!

On balance, when used where they are well suited, engines make a major contribution. On the other hand, if their role is inappropriately overextended, competitiveness, customers' interests and, ultimately, profitability could be jeopardized.

> *"Adverse selection is inherent in human nature. An insurer rarely knows as much about an applicant's medical condition as the applicant does (i.e., symptoms). A proposer for insurance, like a job applicant, will always present the most favorable picture of himself or herself."*
>
> Gordon J. Cramer, FAII

AXA Australia
On The Risk

CHAPTER 10

———•———•———•———•———

Nondisclosure and Antiselection

What is the difference between nondisclosure and antiselection?

These words are often used as synonyms for failure to disclose material information at the time of the application. By "material," we refer to information which would have had an impact, if the underwriter had been aware while assessing the risk, on his final decision regarding insurability.

The distinction between nondisclosure and antiselection comes with regard to intent.

How so?

All antiselection involves nondisclosure, but not all nondisclosure is antiselection. This is because some nondisclosure is inadvertent rather than intentional.

What situations can lead to inadvertent nondisclosure?

1. The question is not understood. Many lay people do not understand even rudimentary medical terminology. This problem is compounded if the application is taken in English and this is

not the applicant's native language.

2. The condition is not covered in the application questions. For example, if the application asks about "disorders of the liver, pancreas or gallbladder" and the applicant's diagnosis was sclerosing cholangitis – a bile duct disorder – he may not acknowledge the impairment because no one asked about "cholangitis" or "bile ducts."

3. The applicant is given a diagnosis which leads him to answer in a manner not reflective of the real risk inherent in his illness. One example would be someone told by his doctor that he just has "a little problem with anemia," when the actual diagnosis, "refractory anemia," is a highly lethal disease once dubbed "preleukemia." The fact that this condition is often discovered inadvertently on routine testing (no symptoms), and also that it is sometimes not treated in its early stages, compound the problem.

4. The application question is not asked properly. This happens mainly on non-medicals. My favorite is: "You don't smoke, do you?" which is a bit different than how we should be asking about tobacco indulgence on the application!

5. The question is not asked at all and a "no" answer is recorded. Sadly, this also happens, albeit rarely (we hope), on non-medical business.

Can we distinguish inadvertent nondisclosure from antiselection?

Usually not at the time the disclosure is made.

Take for example this answer to the application question about "disorder of the colon or rectum":

"Colitis. 6 years ago. OK now."

Obviously, this tells an underwriter almost nothing of value.

Is this answer inadvertent (due to how the question was asked and/or how the applicant's response was recorded)…

...or, is the proposed insured intentionally withholding something that could significantly impact insurability?

How can we minimize inadvertent nondisclosure?

- Ask clearer, better questions on the application.
- In a "perfect world," order medical records on all cases.
- Better use of teleinterviews with drilldown questioning in lieu of traditional application risk questions.

Changing application questions is a time-consuming proposition on a good day.

Increasing our use of the APS would be going in the face of the interests of all parties to the transaction.

Thus, teleinterviews are by far the most logical approach to minimizing inadvertent nondisclosure.

How can we prevent antiselection?

We can't.

However, we can minimize the risk by questioning proposed insureds in more depth when something just doesn't seem to "add up."

We also have the MIB, which is a huge asset in this regard.

Nevertheless, most antiselection is discovered at claim time rather than during the underwriting process.

What is the MIB?

MIB Group, Inc. (MIB) is a membership corporation established to provide coded information to insurers about impairments that applicants have disclosed or that other companies have detected in connection with previous insurance applications.

Are there any recent developments which have increased the risk of antiselection?

Yes, the increasing proliferation of "direct-to-consumer" medical testing.

Is this a big business?

> *"In the next few years, new self-diagnostic technologies that allow people to screen for or manage conditions such as asthma, allergies or congestive heart failure could make this $7 billion global market expand rapidly."*

> Simon Burnell
> Head of Medical Diagnostics
> Cambridge Consultants
> *Clinical Chemistry News*
> March 2008

What does "direct-to-consumer" mean?

Testing where there is no physician involved. Thus, the only way the attending physician can know that such tests were done is if the proposed insured tells him.

What tests are available?

Providers now offer a full range of blood, urine and saliva (oral fluid) tests. I have seen every lab test we currently use for underwriting, except alcohol markers and NT-proBNP, offered by at least one of these firms.

Are these home tests?

For the most part, the fluid specimens are collected at home and sent in for analysis. Where a larger sample – usually blood – is needed, the person goes to a test center offering this service.

In a few cases, the test is self-administered at home and the individual knows the test results immediately.

But the point is that the insured's physician is not involved and, unless the applicant tells his doctor or the insurer about them, there is no "paper trail."

Will these tests lead to antiselection?

It's hard to believe they won't.

For example, if someone has stopped smoking to avoid detection of cotinine (nicotine) in their urine when screened by an insurer, they can buy a test kit to check the urine each day until it is cotinine-free (that is, of course, if that particular test kit is as reliable as the ones insurers use!).

The same would be true if they were heavy drinkers and abstained for a period of time so that telltale tests, if potentially (or known to be) elevated, returned to normal. They could have the same screening tests we use for this purpose done before applying to be sure their period of abstinence had been adequate to realize their attempt at deception.

What can insurers do to minimize this risk?

- Make as much cost-effective use of screening and reflexive lab tests as possible within constraints imposed by their budgets.
- Use screening tests electively below their screening thresholds when aspects of the risk history raise red flags.
- Ask the application/teleinterview question about whether proposed insureds have had any tests done within the past "x" number of years, so that the question encompasses any tests done in addition to those ordered by a medical practitioner.

Are genetic tests also accessible on a direct-to-consumer basis?

Yes.

A growing number of firms have entered this market, offering various combinations of tests for anywhere from a few hundred dollars to as much as $5,000 for a comprehensive genetic marker profile.

How do physicians feel about this practice?

Most dislike it intensely because they are concerned that their patients will misunderstand the implications of test results. The American College of Medical Genetics has gone on record discouraging the use of genetic testing unless done in conjunction with medical care professionals.

Do direct-to-consumer genetic tests pose the same risk for insurers as the non-genetic tests discussed above?

Not yet, because the genetic aspects of the diseases that account for most of our extra mortality and morbidity risk involve many different genes – sometimes hundreds of them – and clinical medicine is a long way from understanding precisely how these tests actually impact the risk of chronic diseases.

CHAPTER 11

———•———•———•———•———

Preparing Your Client For Underwriting

"Taking an insurance case from inception to closing is more often than not a tedious, demanding and frustrating task."

>Ron Verzone
>United Underwriters, Inc.
>Exeter, New Hampshire
>"Between a Rock and a Hard Place"
>*Best's Review*
>April 2008; page 79

Ron is absolutely right! Therefore, we include this chapter to address the steps you can take to eliminate or at least minimize difficulties related to the underwriting portion of this process.

If the application is being done non-medically, what should you do?

The very best job you possibly can when it comes to asking and recording your client's answers to the risk-related questions!

Where the medical questions are concerned, it is essential to make sure all of the following aspects of each condition are addressed.

1. WHAT IS THE IMPAIRMENT?

- Use the most precise name possible.
- For example, if the client says he had "skin cancer," try to pin him down as to the type. There are 3 basic types of skin cancer: basal cell carcinoma, squamous cell carcinoma and malignant melanoma. Which one he had will go a long way to determining insurability.
- The same applies to most other impairments, from kinds of headaches to varieties of hepatitis or colitis, and so on.

2. WHEN WAS IT DIAGNOSED?

- Don't just say "2001" if you also know the month.
- The interval since the diagnosis may directly impact the final underwriting decision.

3. WHAT TESTS WERE DONE TO MAKE THE DIAGNOSIS?

- Knowing what tests the doctor ordered may empower the underwriter to make key inferences as to the degree of risk.
- Be as precise as possible. For example, if the client says doctors used a scope to remove polyps from his colon, ask whether he had sigmoidoscopy (a shorter scope, which can only visualize the last portion of the colon and the rectum) or colonoscopy (which allows the examiner to see the entire colon).

4. WHAT TREATMENT WAS GIVEN?

- If the applicant received medication, we want to know the name of the drug, how it is taken (pill, injection, skin patch, etc.), the actual dosage, and how often it is taken, when he started using it and if he is still taking it. If he stopped using the medication, when and why did he stop?
- If the applicant had surgery, what was the procedure? Were there any complications?

- For all other kinds of treatment: describe what was given or done as precisely as possible and indicate if this treatment relieved the symptoms or cured the problem.

5. WAS THE CLIENT REFERRED TO A SPECIALIST?

- If he was, what was that doctor's specialty?
- When did he first see the specialist, how long was he seen for and when was the last visit?
- Make sure your answers to these other questions also reflect what was done by the specialist as well as the attending physician.
- Make certain you included the name and address of the specialist.

6. WAS YOUR CLIENT TREATED IN A HOSPITAL?

- If yes, was it in an emergency department, as an outpatient or as an inpatient?
- What were the circumstances?
- What tests were done?
- What treatment was given?
- Be sure to include the name and address of the hospital, as well as the name of the doctor who treated him.

7. HAS THERE BEEN ANY RECURRENCE OF THE CONDITION? HAVE THERE BEEN ANY COMPLICATIONS?

- If recurrence: how many times, what were the approximate dates and, most importantly, what was the month and year of the last episode?
- If complications: what were they, how were they treated and are any of them still present?

What if there isn't enough room on the application?

Don't try to squeeze in so much that it becomes impossible to read!

Take another sheet of paper and keep right on going. Just make sure it is dated and signed on the same basis as the application page.

Why do I need to include so much information?

How's this for motivation:

The less the underwriter knows, the more likely he is to require more information to assess insurability.

Therefore, the more you include, the better the odds that the underwriter will make his decision without ordering an APS or medical tests.

Are equivalent questions raised when the medical history is taken paramedically, by an MD or with a teleinterview?

As regards paramedical technicians and examining physicians, the only control insurers have over what they ask is the core questions on the medical history portion of the document they complete. Overall, I can't say that their histories have been superior to the best non-medicals I've seen from skilled producers.

This is precisely why teleunderwriting confers such a huge advantage for you, your client and the insurer. These probing, history-amplifying questions are routinely raised on high quality (which not all of them are) teleinterview drilldown questionnaires. Indeed, the better the quality of drilldown questions, the fewer times underwriters need to get medical records!

What is a "cover letter"?

A communication, usually written, from the producer to the under-writer amplifying and elaborating upon aspects of the case – medical impairment, financial situation, beneficiary designation, insurable interest, etc. – which could have a bearing on how the application is handled by that underwriter.

Is a cover letter a good investment of a producer's time?

Where underwriting is concerned, it may be the BEST investment of his time!

If I were a producer, I would include a cover letter on every case where I could bring additional information to bear that could possibly enhance my client's chances of getting the coverage issued. I would also do this wherever I needed the underwriter's help due to stiff competition.

The more the underwriter knows about the case, the better your chances of a favorable outcome!

Can you cite an example of where a cover letter made an impact?

Sure. Fact is I could cite dozens of them. Here's one of them:

The proposed insured was a middle-aged male. His medical history as he reported it was entirely favorable. However, by underwriting criteria, he was underweight at the time of the paramedical exam.

Knowing that this could disqualify his client for preferred coverage, the producer wrote a cover letter wherein he explained that his client was a devout member of a religion where fasting is required for an extended period at one time of the year. The paramedical just happened to be done at the end of that interval.

Because of this added information from the producer, the underwriter opted to hold off on denying preferred and pursued medical records.

The physician's report affirmed what the producer had reported.

The policy was issued preferred.

Is it ever worth calling the underwriter to get preliminary input before submitting a case?

Absolutely!

You can submit a "trial app" (also called "informal" among other names)...but, unless the case is complex and likely to be substandard or declined, a phone call is faster and usually works just as well.

Be sure that you document the results of the conversation in a cover letter, including the date of the call, what was said and the name of the underwriter.

What should producers do to prepare their client for a paramedical or MD exam?

Exams almost always include blood and urine testing, so I will address both the exam and the tests in my recommendations; see **Hank's 12 Rules of Avoiding Problems on Exams and Tests** on the following page.

All of these factors can lead to avoidable adverse results on physical measurements and/or laboratory tests!

Aren't these rules excessive?

They may seem so, but trust me on this: if you adhere to all 12, you will experience very few avoidable problems related to paramedicals, MD exams as well as routine blood and urine testing.

Perhaps an example will help:

A 55-year-old man in good health and no adverse medical history had a big fight with his wife an hour before his paramedical. He smoked more cigarettes that morning than usual, including 2 within 30 minutes of the exam. When the technician checked his pulse, he had a bunch of premature beats. Based on this, the underwriter ordered an

Hank's 12 Rules for Avoiding Problems on Exams and Tests

1. Get the exam done in the morning wherever possible.

2. Overnight fasting is fine but not essential. Just make sure your client doesn't have blood or urine collected until he has not eaten for at least 2 hours.

3. No cigarette smoking within 1 hour of the exam. Ideally, no tobacco whatsoever for 1 hour.

4. If your client is not diabetic, no change in caffeinated coffee or tea intake that day; he should use the same amount as he does normally. If he is diabetic, abstain from caffeine for at least 2 hours as it may raise his blood sugar.

5. No "energy drinks" the day of the exam.

6. No exercising the morning of the exam.

7. No vigorous exercising within 24 hours.

8. No intensive sports participation – marathon running, long-distance cycling, contact sports, etc. – within 7 days.

9. If your client is ill for any reason, reschedule the appointment.

10. If your client just got out of the hospital as an inpatient, wait a week.

11. If your client is in pain, postpone the exam.

12. If your client has experienced significant agitation or stress within a few hours of the exam, postpone and reschedule. This includes fender-benders, big arguments and so on.

ECG. The ECG showed an unsuspected left bundle branch block. The policy was issued with a hefty rating.

Did the big argument and excess smoking induce the premature beats? We know they can. And what we know for certain is that if there hadn't been premature beats, the LBBB would not have been found and the policy would have been issued smoker-preferred, as applied for.

Do insurers notify applicants of the results of laboratory tests done on them for underwriting purposes?

Some companies send test results directly to applicants; others ask the insured to designate a physician to receive them and then send them to that doctor – and some do neither.

As a rule, I favor the first course of action. But there will be exceptions where it is more prudent to send the test results to the attending physician instead.

Furthermore, I would always send PSA test results – whether abnormal or otherwise – because they should be known to the attending physician so he can correlate them with any PSA tests done clinically.

What can I do if the underwriting file is closed?

There are three main reasons why this happens:

- The application was received incomplete and the missing components did not arrive in the allotted interval.
- One or more requirements did not arrive on time.
- The application was withdrawn.

Find out which one applies in the case at hand and take whatever steps are needed to remedy the situation.

Remember: Applications, exams, tests and even medical reports have a "shelf life," after which they have to be repeated before underwriting can go forward.

Should I ask about reconsideration if action "other than as applied for" is taken on my client's application?

Always!

That is, with the understanding that flat extras and a good share of table ratings are not reconsiderable due to the nature of the impairments.

The same may be true for some individuals denied preferred or placed in a lower preferred category than what they applied for. It depends entirely on the reason(s) why the action was taken.

If reconsideration is possible in the future, what should I do?

- Ask the underwriter when reconsideration is possible.
- Ask what interim evidence – blood pressure rechecks, weight loss, etc. – will be needed to possibly reduce or remove the rating, or allow for a higher class of preferred.
- Get this in writing, just so there is no confusion later on in the event the underwriter has left the company, etc.
- Use this eligibility for reconsideration to leverage delivery of the policy, explaining to your client that by taking the coverage now he is protecting his future insurability. Then, if he does what is required and things turn out favorably, he could be enjoying a lower premium in just a few years' time.

Should I do this if my client is declined?

It depends on whether it was "postpone" declined or "decline" declined!

When we postpone – and we should spell this out – it means we are willing to look again, at some future time and on some basis. This is distinct from a true decline, which means we are unwilling to reconsider our decision in the future.

If it is not clear as to which is true, be sure to clarify.

Then, if it was a postponement, do the same things recommended above for a "not as applied for" final action.

May I appeal if I cannot place the policy because it was not issued as applied for?

Of course.

To whom should my appeal be directed?

Appeals should ALWAYS be directed to the underwriter who made the decision, explaining the basis for your appeal.

What if he turns down my appeal?

Ask the underwriter if he discussed the case with a more experienced underwriter, the medical director and/or the chief underwriter.

If he did, the matter is probably closed unless you ask for an "exception" (and exceptions are being more and more the "exception to the rule" – no pun – nowadays!).

If the underwriter didn't, ask him to get a "second opinion" from one of these other folks.

What if the underwriter refuses?

This seldom happens.

But when it does, you are within your rights to appeal "over his head" if you think you have a valid basis for doing so.

Just remember: When you do this, make sure you exhausted all your options with the underwriter first and also tell him of your intention to appeal up the corporate pecking order BEFORE you proceed.

This may influence his approach.

Here is some sober advice: NEVER alienate the underwriter by handling a situation like this in a less-than-professional manner.

Remember, there are going to be many more cases in the future and nothing good ever comes from intentionally alienating people whose help you may need later on!

What is an exception?

A deviation from the company's usual underwriting practices.

In my view, there are only 2 kinds of exceptions:

- Good exceptions, based on credible information.
- Bad exceptions, done in the absence of credible evidence that they make sense from an underwriting perspective.

For example:

Good Exception: The applicant's coronary risk profile is barely better than average and not favorable enough for super preferred. However, he had a treadmill stress test 4 months prior to the application where he achieved a high level of sustained exercise with completely normal results. In most cases, I would think this would bump him up a level in this context.

Bad Exception: The same applicant does not have equivalent justification for being moved up to a higher level of preferred, but the underwriter does so anyway.

CHAPTER 11

———•———•———•———•———

Financial Underwriting
DuWayne Kilbo, MBA FLMI

"Show me the money!"

Jerry Maguire, The Movie (1996)

We all know that financial underwriting has gotten tough out there….

A few years ago it was relatively easy to get a case financially underwritten, no matter what the face amount. All you had to do was come up with a few scant pieces of financial information, and magically an app was financially approved.

Yeah, times were great and things were simple.

But that was then, this is now….

Financial underwriting is back in vogue and it's come back with a painful vengeance.

What happened?

Reinsurance/retrocessionaire admonishment and loss of appetite for large face amount cases (especially at the older ages), Investor/Stranger Owned Life Insurance (IOLI/STOLI), carrier acknowledgement of financial underwriting laxity, and a mix of other things have all added up to make financial underwriting more difficult.

And with what the industry has been through during the past few years, considering IOLI/STOLI and other marketing schemes, perhaps the perfect storm of change was overdue....

At one time Inspection Reports (IR) and Personal History Interviews (PHI) provided the bulk of the planning and financial information needed to get a case through underwriting.

Not any more.

Today, it is necessary to have all financial information and other facts together to get a case through underwriting.

We're finding it typical for carriers to request and even require – especially at the larger face amounts and older ages:

- Signed financial questionnaires that become part of the policy
- Signed purpose of insurance forms, including all loan forms, term sheets and supporting schedules if premium financing is being considered
- Copies of tax statements with all supporting schedules, verifying income and sources of income and ability to pay the policy premium
- 3rd party financial statements along with supporting source documents verifying all assets, liabilities and net worth
- Business financials, with balance sheet, profit and loss statement, and all supporting schedules for the past couple years
- Complete trust documents
- Planning documents

On top of this, carriers are demanding (yes, DEMANDING!) cover memos explaining need and purpose of coverage.

Wow!!!

It's "Show Me the Money" time – and not only where the money is currently, but where it will be in the future and how and why it will be there. The onus is clearly on the producer to demonstrate all of this to a carrier.

We can all agree that times have changed. And we can also safely assume that things aren't going back to the old ways any time soon.

Let's review where we are today and what we need to get an application financially underwritten and approved.

First, let's start by going through a refresher on some "basics" of financial underwriting, and then we'll press on to more specific financial information that can be used to get cases underwritten and approved.

THE BASICS

Why is financial underwriting important?

Like two sides of the same coin, medical and financial underwriting share the same objective and are critical to meeting carrier mortality assumptions. And financial underwriting is just as important as medical underwriting, if not more important at times.

Since financial underwriting is not an exact science, most carriers are not willing to go on record to say exactly when adverse financial underwriting selection (aka: antiselection) occurs. Adverse selection can occur in the first year to several years after a policy is issued. However, most claims are believed due to unnatural deaths such as suicide, traumatic, or accidental deaths.

It's important for carriers to get financial underwriting right since it only takes a couple of hiccups to skew mortality results.

Do smaller or larger face amounts carry more financial underwriting risk?

While larger face amounts – those over a few million – are traditionally scrutinized more heavily in terms of financial underwriting, adverse financial underwriting experience can and does occur at any face amount.

Whether it's a $50,000 or a $100 million plus policy, a few extra or over-insured deaths here or there add up in a hurry, no matter what the face amount.

So why should we care?

Excess mortality due to adverse financial concerns doesn't necessarily bode well for carriers, producers, insureds, reinsurers or the industry, since it can and will translate into higher mortality charges down the road. Most carriers have the ability to raise mortality rates on in-force coverage, as long as it is done across the board on an entire block of business.

Doesn't sound good, does it?

This is a black eye that no one wants or can afford.

If we're in this industry for the long haul, which you likely are if you are reading this book, then we must care....

What is financial underwriting?

In underwriting terms: it's a review of insurable interest, purpose of coverage, owner/beneficiary arrangement, amount requested, financial information, and other financial or non-financial information, and determining what loss occurs and the magnitude of that loss if a person should die.

OK...saying it in simpler terms: whether the coverage is for business, personal or other purposes, it's simply verifying that insurable interest exists and that we are not making someone worth more dead than alive.

Financial underwriting is also necessary to ensure there will not be excess early lapse rates.

Pricing of life insurance coverage typically takes into account a certain level of policy lapsation, which ultimately translates into non-claims payment down the road. This helps to make coverage more affordable for all insureds. However, excess early lapsation – typically within 5 years of policy issue – causes carrier financial loss due to limited recovery of policy acquisition cost.

Makes sense, doesn't it? Provide coverage but only enough to assure the continued life of an insured. Once coverage is put in force, make sure that it will stay in force for the foreseeable future.

Over the past few years another major reason has come about for doing financial underwriting, and this is to make sure that coverage applied for isn't part of a STOLI/IOLI or other prearranged settlement market "flip" transaction.

The target market for this type of coverage is in the mid-70s and older age group. If the premium for coverage applied for appears to be beyond the financial means of an insured—no matter if the face amount is financially justified—the carriers will seek further explanation or refuse to issue coverage.

What makes insurable interest so critical?

The owner and/or beneficiary must suffer an emotional and/or financial loss upon the death of the insured. If this does not occur, then there is no insurable interest and the insurance contract may be considered wagering and invalid.

Bottom line, there has to be insurable interest...ALWAYS. Make sure it is present. If not, you will get immediate pushback from your underwriter.

So who has insurable interest and how much is deemed to exist?

It depends. For example:

- Typically immediate family members such as a spouse, child, parent, etc., have insurable interest in the life of one another. The amount depends upon the financial background of the insured and possibly family wealth.
- Co-debtors have insurable interest in one another to the extent of their debt obligation.
- A charity may have insurable interest in a key donor.
- A bank has insurable interest in the principals or primary movers of a business up to a portion of an outstanding business loan.
- A business has insurable interest in business partners for buy-sell coverage up to the economic value each partner has in the business. This is also true for key person coverage. A business has economic interest in a key person up to the amount that the person's unique skills are difficult to replace, measurable and contribute to business success.

Does insurable interest need to be present after issue?

Insurable interest must be present at time of issue. There has been some debate on whether it needs to be present after issue, since a life insurance policy is defined as property by most every state and is able to be transferred and sold.

There have been recent court cases challenging after-issue insurable interest changes, primarily as it relates to STOLI/IOLI or prearranged flip transactions. In these situations insurable interest is "manufactured" to be present at time of issue. However, at some time after issue the owner/beneficiary on the policy is changed and insurable interest is not present. Carriers have looked at these situations closely, and in certain situations have rescinded coverage and charged back commission based upon material misrepresentation. In addition, there is some effort recently to consider these transactions to be fraudulent, whereby the 2 year contestability period does not apply, coverage is rescinded *and* premiums paid on the policy are retained by the insurance carrier.

Insurable interest is important!

What do carriers look at when financial underwriting?

There are several things that underwriters consider when reviewing an application. However, the most common things reviewed and considered are:

- **APPLICATION:** This provides basic demographic information, in force and applied for coverage, insured/owner/beneficiary information, purpose of coverage, and relatively modest financial information. This is usually the only thing required on a simple, straightforward case with a face amount in the hundreds of thousands. For applications with face amounts in the millions, there are several other additional things typically required, such as financial supplements and other signed disclosures.

- **TRUST DOCUMENTS AND APPLICATION ADDENDA:** IOLI/STOLI ushered in a variety of additional required carrier application forms. Depending on carrier, applications as low as $1 million in face amount and starting at age 65 may require additional signed/dated disclosure forms regarding income, worth and purpose of coverage. If premium financing is being pursued, the terms and details of the financing arrangement are also requested, as well as other information such as financing documents and trust documents. Trust documents are required by most carriers for trusts established within the past couple of years—especially at the older ages. The trust document usually goes through a carrier review process to make sure there isn't anything unusual that suggests IOLI/STOLI coverage or a similar arrangement. The signed application forms ultimately become part of the insurance contract once coverage is issued and are contestable should a material non-disclosure be discovered at a later date.

- **Cover Memo:** This is an absolute must when submitting large face amount applications with tens of thousands in premium, or when there is something unusual that can't be explained via normal insurance application questions/declarations. Insurance applications are notoriously ill-equipped to handle the detail required for some insureds, and it is not advisable to risk a 6 figure commission on the answers to ordinary application questions. It is easier to put an underwriter in the proper frame of mind with details of the sale, rather than to overcome an objection based upon some misunderstood piece of information. Underwriters typically want to help and approve coverage. We need to give them reasons to issue coverage, and a cover memo does the job nicely.

- **Source of Business:** Underwriters consider very carefully the source of business when reviewing applications. If you establish yourself as a reputable source of business with a history of full disclosure, it is almost guaranteed that cases will be underwritten quicker and with fewer questions and hassles. If you haven't done so, pick up the phone and work closely with your underwriter(s) to develop a positive image and reputation of yourself that they can count on. If possible, pay them a visit. Your underwriters need to know you, and you need to know them. It will be well worth your time to do so.

- **PHIs & IRs:** As you know, in large case situations, carriers or their contracted inspection services call applicants directly and ask them a series of questions. Some questions may have already been asked via the application. However, some questions may be new to the applicant. They do this to confirm and clarify information already received. Additional questions asked, especially to older-age applicants, include purpose of coverage, whether there was any discussion about selling a policy after it is issued, if there was an offer of free insurance, how premiums will be paid, and if there was upfront money offered by a third party. Applicants typically are very candid during phone calls and an unbelievable amount of financial and other information is available from direct client interviews. In addition, other references may be contacted, including an applicant's banking and accounting sources. With any discussion of PHIs and IRs, it is important to note that most people don't like to disclose financial information to an unknown person – especially over the phone. In large case situations, it is best to tell your clients that someone will be calling to confirm financial and other application information. If they aren't comfortable disclosing financial information over the phone, then simply submit written financial confirmation directly to the underwriter and inform the carrier not to ask for financial verification during the PHI or IR.

- **INTERNET:** If you haven't already done so, go to the Internet and "Google" your name. You may be very surprised at the information available on you via the internet! Underwriters routinely use the Internet when something is unusual or they are seeking additional financial or other information about an insured. The wise producer will do their own Internet search, both to uncover additional favorable information about their clients and to know if there is any unknown information that needs to be addressed prior to carrier submission of an application.

- **FINANCIAL STATEMENTS:** Third party financial statements, verified by an accountant or attorney, are the "gold standard" of financial underwriting. In large face amount applications, beginning at face amounts of $5 to $10 million (depending upon age of applicant), carriers ask for all assets, liabilities and net worth to be broken down and verified in a written third party statement. In addition they may require copies of supporting source documents such as brokerage account statements, addresses of all properties and businesses owned in order to verify ownership, etc. At times it is difficult to get a third party statement, simply because a client hasn't gone through the time and expense of having a certified public accountant (CPA) compile their financial statement. Also, due to accounting standards and potential malpractice issues, accountants are reluctant to sign off on statements where they have not personally examined and certified a client's assets and liabilities. In these situations, other third party information such as brokerage and bank statements that detail a majority of net worth are suitable. Internet searches that detail items such as company and stock ownership also work. If residential real estate is substantial, there are Internet sources such as zillow.com that provide real estate values for most every area of the country. For large face amount business insurance application, two years of the most recent audited business financial statements are usually requested, including a balance sheet, profit and loss statement and all supporting schedules. If the business is relatively new, the most current available unaudited financial statements are usually acceptable. However, the information should be complete as possible. A good idea with any business coverage application, and especially for a relatively new business, is to include an overview and resume of all key people in the business. This helps the underwriter understand the key players and their potential for business success. If an application is for key person coverage and a large face amount, an individual 1040 form or other tax forms may be requested. If coverage is for loan coverage, the terms of the loan need to be disclosed. And at larger face amounts, actual loan papers may be required.

- **TAX STATEMENTS:** In the past, third party verified financial statements via an accountant or attorney were sufficient for large face amount situations, and tax statements were only required when there were financial discrepancies that needed to be resolved. Today, and as another side effect of IOLI/STOLI – especially at the older ages – carriers routinely ask for tax statements to verify ability to pay policy premiums. However, as we all know, tax statements are sometimes misleading, especially in situations where there is business ownership. In these situations, and for obvious reasons, taxable income is often kept as low as possible. A discussion with the underwriter is necessary in these situations to clear up any issues that may arise.

Beyond the Basics

The discussion up to this point has been on some of the basics of financial underwriting. We will now discuss more specific things that you can use to get your cases financially underwritten and approved.

We will discuss things your underwriters look at when financially underwriting cases – such as formulas and financial information – to determine if the amount of coverage requested is within their underwriting limits and guidelines.

Both personal and business-needs coverage will be addressed. We will finish up with a discussion on premium financing and some of the issues faced with this type of coverage.

How were financial underwriting rules and guidelines developed?

Financial underwriting rules and guidelines developed over the years, some through old English laws enacted in the 1700's that make it illegal to gamble or wager on one's life, to more current legislation. Others evolved through trial and error, as well as common sense.

Are underwriting rules and guidelines consistent amongst carriers?

Historically, reinsurers have been a major driver of financial underwriting guidelines and rules, since they have a large block of in-force business, and experience excess mortality associated with things such as over-insurance. Through their reinsurance agreements, they are able to dictate direct carrier financial underwriting guidelines. In view of this, most carriers are fairly consistent in their approach to financial underwriting. However, there are outliers, especially with large retention carriers who may apply their guidelines and rules more aggressively in certain situations.

What about group coverage? Do carriers take that into account when financial underwriting?

Group coverage tends to be very modest in face amount—in the $50,000 to $200,000 range —and is typically a small multiple of income. Most carriers acknowledge group coverage, but will disregard it if modest or a small percentage of the overall insurance need.

Underwriting Personal Needs Coverage

Personal needs coverage comprises the majority of coverage applied for in the life industry. This coverage is primarily used for income replacement, estate conservation and personal loan coverage needs.

What is income replacement coverage?

Income replacement coverage is intended to replace income due to the untimely death of a breadwinner or primary wage earner. The death benefits are intended to flow directly to an insured's heirs to cover things such as food, shelter, medical expenses, educational costs, spouse's retirement, pay off debt, and many other things.

How is the maximum income replacement coverage arrived at?

There are many ways to determine the maximum income replacement coverage. Most are based on simplistic tables or formulas that prescribe a future value multiplication factor of current income tied to an applicant's age.

The future value factor is multiplied against the applicant's current earned income to arrive at the amount of income lost due to an untimely death. This provides the ultimate, maximum death benefit for which one may qualify.

On the following page is an example of a typical income replacement table:

Age of Applicant	Income Multiplication Factor
Up to 30	30
31-40	25
41-50	20
51-55	15
56-65	10
66-70	5-7
Over 70	Underwriter Discretion. Typically not more than 5 times if still working

For example, if an applicant is age 50 and earns $100,000 per year, he may qualify for a maximum total line of $2 million of coverage: $100,000 x 20 (income factor at age 50) = $2 million.

Here's an example of an income replacement formula used in the industry today:

STEP 1: (age 70 minus current age)(.7) = Income replacement factor.
STEP 2: (Income Factor)(Annual Income) = Maximum income
        replacement need.

For example, our age 50 person earning $100,000 per year has an income replacement factor of 14, and a total personal insurance need of $1.4 million:

(70-50)(.7) = 14, (14 x $100,000) = $1,400,000.

What happens if a person applies for coverage over these limits?

As noted above, the different income replacement approaches yield slightly different results – given a similar set of facts. If an applicant is applying for $1.5 million of coverage and has no coverage in force – for a total line of $1.5 million of coverage – one carrier may believe the proposed insured may be over-insured, while the other believes he is well within their income replacement guidelines.

Most carriers will allow for some "overage" beyond their tables or formulas, especially if the proposed insured is in good health. Also, if there is reason to believe earned income will increase substantially in the upcoming years (rather than remain static), and this is effectively communicated to the underwriter, then there is a good chance that a carrier may allow their income factors to be exceeded.

It is important to know each carrier's financial underwriting guidelines since they may be different. This will cause you fewer headaches and hassles when submitting applications to a variety of carriers.

How much overage will a carrier typically allow?

Five to ten percent is a common acceptable factor for overage without further explanation. For example, if the proposed insured is eligible for $1.4 million of coverage but needs $1.5 million, this is typically acceptable ($100,000, or 7% over maximum income replacement guidelines).

Are there are other issues to consider for income replacement coverage?

Yes. There are several additional items to keep in mind:

Insurers only consider a proposed insured's earned – versus unearned – income when determining maximum coverage amounts.

- Earned income includes those things that will cease at the death of an insured. It is defined as one's gross income before taxes and other deductions, and is the amount of gross income noted on a 1040 form. For Sub Chapter S, Sole Proprietor and Partnership income recipients, it is the proposed insured's bottom line income, after expenses. Earned income includes regular recurring bonuses, commissions if they are stable, some profit sharing arrangements, stock options, and the value of company benefits such as auto and housing.

- Unearned income is not considered for income replacement, since this income will continue after the death of an insured. It includes capital gains, some dividends if they continue beyond death, rental income, interest income, expense reimbursement, and any other income which may not cease at death.

Also, you've heard it before and you'll hear it again and again, *provide cover memos*!

This is an absolute must when submitting large face amount applications with several thousands in premium, or when there is something unusual that can't be explained through normal insurance application questions/declarations. Put your underwriter at ease and in a proper frame of mind when reviewing your applications.

Do not jeopardize the outcome on something that will only take you a few minutes to handle in a cover memo!

What about coverage on dependent spouses?

Dependent spouses are eligible for coverage, even if they don't work. Typically the face amount of coverage is based upon a reasonable estimate of long-term replacement for such things as the homemaking and child care. Face amounts of $200,000 to $300,000 are common.

Occasionally the face amounts may approach up to one-half of the face amount of coverage in-force or applied for on the working spouse, and assuming an adequate explanation is provided, the face amount may be several hundred thousand to millions in face amounts. The carriers will require that the working spouse be adequately insured (assuming he or she is in reasonable health) prior to approving coverage on a dependent spouse.

What about coverage on children?

Other than final expense needs, there typically isn't a large need for coverage on children. Face amounts up to $50,000 are common.

However, there is an occasional need for coverage beyond these amounts.

Due to the life insurance tax wrapper, the low mortality charges on juveniles, and the large accumulation potential provided by variable life and other accumulation life insurance products, large face amount life insurance is being applied for on children. Most of this coverage is for future college expenses and other accumulation needs. These situations are typically "OK" with the carriers as long as the parents are adequately insured—with OK being defined by the carriers. Typically the face amount cannot exceed the amount of in-force coverage on the least-insured parent. In addition, all children within a family should be equally insured or have equally funded insurance plans.

How about inheritable worth coverage on children?

Rarely will carriers consider inheritable worth coverage on children. However, if a child has a large amount of assets titled in their name, there may be a need for a large amount of coverage to cover their estate tax needs. In these situations it is necessary to clearly demonstrate a need for coverage via net worth statements, trust documents, any other financial planning information available, ***and a good cover memo***.

What is estate conservation coverage?

Estate conservation coverage is intended to cover the final expenses and taxes associated with one's estate upon death.

The erosion of an estate can be significant, approaching over 50% of estate value when considering Federal, State and other final expenses. An untimely death can also cause a forced sell of assets, which can further deplete the value of an estate.

In the more advanced planning situations, an Irrevocable Life Insurance Trust (ILIT) is drawn up to keep the life insurance proceeds outside of the insured's estate and to cover final estate expenses. Premiums are gifted to the trust to pay premiums. If there are two living spouses, last survivor coverage is typically the plan of choice due to the low cost of insurance charges for the joint insureds and the unlimited marital deduction. However, there may be first death needs as well, so individual life coverage also makes sense.

How is the maximum estate conservation coverage determined?

The eligible amount of estate coverage is primarily based upon net worth. Net worth consists of all personal assets minus liabilities. Assets include items such as property, stocks, bonds, marketable securities, jewelry, art work, automobiles, aircraft and business ownership. Mortgages and loans are examples of liabilities.

After net worth is calculated, future estate growth may be applied to this figure with the ultimate amount multiplied by an estate tax rate to determine estate conservation need.

Here is an example of an estate conservation formula:

{(Net Worth)(Future Value Interest Factor)}(Estate Tax Rate of 55%)

What is a Future Value Interest Factor (FVIF)?

Depending upon age of the proposed insured, carriers typically allow estate growth into their calculation of estate value.

To determine the amount of growth, carriers apply a future value factor, which consists of an interest rate and years of growth.

Interest rates vary by carriers, but it is common to see growth factors in the 5% to 7% range. The greater growth percentage is used on estates that have greater appreciation potential due to rapidly growing assets, such as a high growth business, investment portfolios and some real estate.

In regard to the number of years of growth, some carriers use up to one-half life expectancy for a growth factor, especially with last survivor plans of coverage, while others use more limited numbers as suggested in the table below:

Age	Years of Growth
55 & Under	10 to 15 years
56 to 65	7-10 years
66 and over	The lesser of 7 years to one-half life expectancy

Why is 55%* used for the estate tax rate?

This also varies amongst carriers, with numbers being as low as 45% to as high as 60%. As indicated earlier, financial underwriting is an inexact science so the estate tax rate only needs to be close. In view of this, a 55% estate tax rate is adequate for most carriers. This rate covers both Federal and State estate and final tax needs.

Using the formula above, if a person is age 65 and has an estate worth $10 million, he will qualify for $9.85 million of estate needs coverage:

{$10 million)(1.7908, which is the Future Value Interest Factor at 6% and 10 years of growth)}(Estate Tax Rate of 55%) = $9.85 million

* *The 55% rate as well as the current federal estate tax exemption may change with the newly elected Federal Administration and Congress. At present, the conventional wisdom is that the estate tax rate will decrease and the estate tax exemption will increase. If and when either of these occur, the estate conservation formula will be modified to reflect current estate taxation policy.*

Is this the maximum coverage available for estate tax needs?

Yes. However, as in income replacement coverage, some overage is acceptable.

Is estate conservation coverage offset by the amount of income replacement coverage?

No. These are two entirely different needs, and estate and income replacement coverage may be stacked.

What about overlapping coverage situations?

When determining estate coverage, be careful to take into account overlapping personal and business needs coverage. Personal worth covered by life insurance for business purposes may not necessarily need to be covered again for estate conservation purposes.

It makes sense…The asset may already be insured through business coverage so there is no need to insure it again. For example, a buy-sell agreement may provide life insurance coverage in case one of the business partners dies. In this situation, there may not be a need to include the value of the business as part of personal net worth for estate conservation needs. The business worth is essentially payable as death benefits to an insured's heirs via his business needs coverage. For example, if a business is worth $10 million and the total estate is worth $30 million including the business, then the net estate eligible for estate conservation coverage is $20 million.

What things do the carriers require to verify net worth?

For applications with face amounts up to $5 to $10 million, most carriers will use application disclosures; supplemental application forms that break down personal assets, income and liabilities; and PHI/IR disclosures.

For amounts greater than these, the carriers typically require documented and signed third party verified financial information by a CPA or estate planning attorney.

What if my client doesn't have a third party verified financial statement available?

It occurs with some frequency that some people, even very wealthy people, do not have a third party financial statement. In many situations they are not willing to get an accountant or others to verify their worth due to the fact that the cost is significant. In addition, CPAs are typically prevented from verifying worth without having audited the individual assets and liabilities of the proposed insured.

What should I do if a third party statement isn't available?

There are acceptable alternatives in these situations. Carriers are willing to accept tax forms, brokerage statements, business financial statements (where a large portion of wealth is tied up in a business), property tax statements and other surrogates to verify large portions of wealth.

There is also an abundant amount of personal information available on the Internet, such as stock ownership information, business information, home values and property values that will help verify net worth.

Why do carriers ask for so much financial and other information when my applicant is age 65 or 70?

Insurers are absolutely paranoid about being a party to an IOLI/SOLI transaction!

Since most of this business occurs in the over-70 age group, they ask for much more detailed financial information. Tax forms, detailed disclosure forms and verified financial information, property information and all supporting source documents are commonly requested. This information helps the carriers sort through and thus ascertain if the applicant has the ability to pay premiums, is worth what they say, and whether he may be involved in an investor-initiated transaction.

Are there other issues to consider for estate conservation coverage?

Absolutely!

Provide a cover memo!

Don't risk your livelihood on something that can be handled by the few minutes it takes to draft a memo. Put your underwriter at ease and in the proper frame of mind when reviewing your applications. Include details about the client's background, and let them know your expectations so these can be managed appropriately.

What is personal loan coverage?

Personal loan coverage should not be confused with loan coverage for business needs.

Typically, personal loan insurance is for covering an outstanding mortgage balance, and may be required by a lender. Term insurance is typically the coverage of choice in these situations.

How is the maximum loan coverage amount arrived at?

Typically the face amount requested is consistent with the outstanding loan balance, with a joint primary beneficiary designation listing a personal beneficiary and the name of the lender "as interests may appear."

Underwriting Business Needs Coverage

Business needs is the other major category of insurance applied for in the life industry. While this coverage takes many forms, we will discuss the most common ones which are buy-sell or stock redemption coverage, key person, deferred compensation and loan coverage.

The difference between business and personal needs coverage is that the business has some type of economic interest in the life of the insured, and the death of the insured causes a financial loss for the business or its surviving partners.

What is buy-sell or stock redemption coverage?

This type of coverage is used by living business partner(s) to purchase the business interest from the estate of a deceased partner.

The buy-sell agreement details the terms of death benefit distribution. This coverage eliminates uncertainty around business transfer surrounding potential outsiders and personal heirs to the business, who may lack both knowledge and ability to run the business successfully or feel a need to liquidate or sell their share of the business. The deceased partner's heirs receive life insurance proceeds for their business share.

This coverage is also called stock redemption coverage if used for stock shareholders of a business. There is an agreement between the corporation and its shareholders in these situations.

Should all business partners be insured?

Absolutely! All partners must be insured for a face amount consistent with their ownership share. The carriers look at this very closely to be sure there is no antiselection occurring with the applied-for coverage, which may happen if coverage is only being applied for on a single partner.

How are amounts of coverage determined?

The amount of coverage is a function of business valuation and the percentage ownership in the business of each partner.

How does the underwriter determine business value?

Typically the business value is determined by some type of valuation methodology, or the business may have had its market value established by an independent valuation firm.

Determining business value is easy if valued by an independent firm, as long as the assumptions in the valuation report appear reasonable.

If the business has not been given a market value, things get a bit more challenging. In these situations, some type of written rationale in the form of a cover memo regarding business valuation must be provided to the underwriter. Supplementary application forms, IRs and PHIs that further detail various business financial figures may also be requested.

If the coverage requested is sufficiently large, in the several million dollar range, then supporting financial documentation should accompany the cover memo. Sometimes it may be necessary to include the most recent two years of balance sheets, income statements, and supporting schedules.

The underwriter, with your help, will look at the documentation provided and determine an appropriate business value based upon a few different business valuation methodologies.

The most common methods for business valuation include:

- **BOOK VALUE.** This is simply the assets of the business minus its liabilities, and it most often understates business value.

- **MARKET VALUE.** What the business may be worth if sold on the open market. Often it is an educated guess based on like businesses in a similar industry. If the market value is within 20% to 25% of the book value of the business, the amount is usually accepted without further discussion. The underwriter looks at the reasonableness of the value suggested based upon such things as company goodwill – which is the amount of value being suggested above book value – years the company has been in business, Internet sources detailing values of like businesses in a similar industry and other things.

- **CAPITALIZATION OF EARNINGS.** This method attempts to get at market value by using a multiplication factor against bottom line business earnings. Companies that have been in business for quite some time and are stable may have an earnings factor of 12 to 16 times net income, versus a new business that may have an earnings factor of 3 to 4 times. For example, if an old established business has a bottom line income of $1 million, then the estimated business market value of the business is $12 to 16 million ($1 million x 12 -16 earnings factor).

Which of the business valuation methodologies does an underwriter typically use?

There is no set rule on which valuation method an underwriter will use.

Most often they will use the valuation method that yields the greatest business value – if there is a good rational reason provided by the producer to do so. If there isn't a good rationale provided, then an average of the three methodologies may be done, and a business value within 10% to 20% of the average of the three methodologies is usually acceptable.

Are there any other things to consider?

Yes. ***Provide a memo!***

Buy-sell coverage is usually a big ticket item, and is typically wrapped up with other sales such as key man and estate conservation coverage. Don't risk a terrific multimillion dollar face amount sale and thousands to hundreds of thousands of premium on what the application disclosures may provide your underwriter. Give additional business details and background to put your underwriter at ease. It is well worth your time.

What is key person coverage?

Key person coverage is intended to financially protect a business from the loss of a person critical to business success. It helps replace the financial loss associated with the death of a key business person and skill necessary for business success.

Who may be a key person?

A key person may include high producing and successful sales people, business owners, officers of a corporation, research and development personnel and other uniquely talented or difficult to replace individuals.

The critical elements of a key person are that their skills are not easily replaced, they are critical to business success, and their death will cause a significant financial loss for the company. The key person coverage will help cover recruiting and training costs for a replacement, help the business operate while a replacement is being found, and help with any outstanding loan obligations.

An officer of a company may be a key person. Conversely, an assembly line worker is not a key person.

Do all key people in similar positions need to be insured?

Absolutely! Your underwriter will look at this closely. This is a flag for antiselection if all people in similar positions are not insured in a like manner. If and when this occurs a solid explanation needs to be provided to the underwriter to make them feel comfortable with the sale.

How are key person amounts arrived at?

Typically the amount of key person coverage is a function of salary, with the face amount of coverage requested being in the range of 5 to 10 times salary.

For example, if a key person's salary is $100,000, they may qualify for between $500,000 and $1 million of coverage depending upon how "key" the person is to business success.

The differentiators for amount of coverage include the number of years the business has been in operation, number of employees, amount of time the key person has been with the company, age of the key person, stability of company, and the critical skills provided by the key person.

If coverage applied for is within these ranges, your underwriter will usually approve the application without additional explanation, unless coverage applied for is very high – in the several million dollar range.

Amounts above 10 times income may be acceptable if there is adequate explanation and financial detail provided. For example, a person who earns $750,000 per year and who is responsible for bringing $10 million in gross revenues annually to an investment firm may be eligible for much more than $7.5 million of key man coverage. In this situation, a 1 to 2 time multiple of earnings may be appropriate. The key is to provide a good sound explanation for the sale to help your underwriter understand the need.

How is a key person valued for start-up businesses?

Start-up businesses are challenging for any type of business coverage, whether it be for buy-sell, key person or other needs. The critical elements in these situations are for the key people to have a prior track record of success and the critical skill set necessary for business success.

However, be aware that your underwriter may be very conservative in these situations until a successful 1 to 2 year business track record is established.

Who are the owner and beneficiary of key person coverage?

The business is the owner and beneficiary, since it will suffer the loss.

What is loan coverage?

Loan coverage is called many things: debt protection, creditor insurance, loan coverage, and bank coverage.

Loan coverage is intended to cover outstanding debt associated with a business. This may include debt associated with bank financing of new equipment, or debt associated with borrowing for business development. Whatever the case, there is a debt that requires repayment to a lender.

Although the reasons are not totally clear, of all the different types of business coverage issued – buy-sell, key man, loan coverage, etc. – loan coverage typically has the highest associated mortality. In view of this, underwriters look very carefully at these applications for coverage.

Who is usually insured for loan coverage?

The ultimate drivers of the business – such as business owners – are the most common insureds for loan coverage. The key is for the insured to have a significant stake in business success and ultimate responsibility for the loan amount.

How are face amounts determined for loan coverage?

The face amount is a function of the outstanding loan balance. However, carriers usually do not insure the full amount of the loan or loan balance. They usually offset the loan amount by up to 30 percent, and cover the rest. Their rationale is that they will achieve better mortality and persistency results if the business also has some skin in the game.

Is there a minimum length for the loan period?

The carriers require a loan period of at least 5 to 7 years. Anything shorter than this is not profitable for the carriers. They are not able to pay commission and recover acquisition cost in a shorter time period.

Are there any other things my underwriter may consider for loan coverage?

Yes.

They may look at the profitability of the business and whether it has the ability to pay back the loan. This is usually determined via loan documents and business financial statements when the face amount requested is in the few to several million dollar ranges. More modest amounts of coverage typically are qualified by application disclosures and perhaps PHI reports, and don't require a great amount of information for underwriting purposes.

What is deferred compensation coverage?

Deferred compensation coverage is a perk for key people or key drivers of a business. Life insurance, because of its tax wrapper and accumulation potential, is often used for deferred compensation for key people upon retirement or some other event.

Deferred compensation coverage is often used to create "golden handcuffs" for people who are key to business success so they will remain with the business long-term.

There are also other types of coverage that fall under the underwriting label of deferred compensation, such as executive bonus and retirement health benefits. This coverage also follows the underwriting rules and guidelines of deferred compensation.

How are deferred compensation amounts determined?

Amounts are usually a function of income, with the face amount of deferred compensation coverage being up to 10 times the salary and other perks of the insured.

Who gets the death benefits if a person should die?

Upon death of the insured, the business usually gets the sum of the premiums paid to date for the insurance, with the balance of benefits going to the personal beneficiaries of the insured.

Do all people in a similar position need to have deferred compensation coverage in force?

Yes.

Underwriters are very particular about coverage being selectively applied for on people. Their antennae go up when amounts are unequally or inconsistently applied for on a similar class of employee. If this should occur, a cover memo detailing how amounts were determined is in order. Again, put your underwriter at ease and in the proper frame of mind when reviewing your cases.

UNDERWRITING PREMIUM FINANCE COVERAGE

Everyone – underwriters, producers, new business and compliance – struggles with coverage that is premium financed!

Carriers have been underwriting this type of coverage for several years and without issue. However, during the past few years, IOLI/STOLI and prearranged flip transactions have crept into the premium financing shelf space and have ushered in an entirely new era in underwriting challenges. Underwriting shops are taking extra care to be sure they are accepting quality premium finance arrangements and are weeding out unwanted programs.

Because of IOLI/STOLI and prearranged flip sales, an increased level of application due diligence has occurred with underwriting and compliance departments reviewing trust documents, disclosure forms, and financing details, particularly in the 70-plus age applicants. There are additional questions being asked on inspection reports confirming such things as the purpose of coverage, if there was discussion about a policy sale, and if upfront money is being considered as an inducement to buy the policy. Data mining software has been developed for carriers to review entire blocks of in-force business to uncover adverse trends. Calls are being made by carrier compliance areas to applicants and financiers prior to policy issue to determine the nature of the premium financing arrangement. And random after-issue "customer satisfaction" calls are being made to applicants to question them about the nature of the sale and uncover what was discussed during the sales process.

There is acceptable premium financing and unacceptable premium financing. It's extremely wise and prudent to provide full disclosure, and not cross the line to unacceptable premium financing!

The end result of application nondisclosure for sales that look and smell like IOLI/STOLI and flip transactions is that litigation ensues, producers and production groups are fired, reputations are forever lost, policies are rescinded and commission chargebacks occur – many in the hundreds of thousands to millions of dollars range.

This is SERIOUS STUFF with SERIOUS IMPLICATIONS!

It pays to do premium financing right, and to only do premium financing with carriers that will accept this type of coverage.

Why would one consider premium financing?

There are several valid reasons to consider premium financing. Typically, premium financing is considered in large face amount sales, and usually this occurs at the older ages, above age 70, where premiums are substantial.

Some common reasons for premium financing include:

- To keep the death benefits outside of one's estate, typically an insurance trust is developed that is the owner and beneficiary of coverage. However, money must be given or granted to the trust to fund premiums. Because the trust is a separate legal entity, the monies granted are considered a gift and may invoke gift taxes if beyond the acceptable annual gifting limits, or cause use of one's lifetime exemption which an applicant may want to preserve for other estate planning needs.

- One's estate may be illiquid, such as in real estate. In this situation, the applicant doesn't want to sell their property to pay premiums.

- An applicant's personal assets may be generating a greater return than the cost of premium financing, such as in a stock portfolio or business investment. In view of this positive arbitrage, they can pay the note without liquidating assets to pay premiums.

- The insured has a sizeable estate but may have a cash flow crunch at the time coverage is applied for. This situation requires short-term premium financing as a means to pay the premium. At a future date, when cash flow is improved, the premium financing agreement will be retired.

What financing arrangements do the carriers typically accept?

Many premium finance arrangements are the "traditional," full recourse type of loan where the owner/insured has "skin in the game" – i.e., fully collateralized borrowing and periodic interest paid on the note – whether it be monthly, quarterly, semiannually, or annually. Sometimes interest may be rolled into the note, depending upon lender and carrier requirements. Acceptable collateral requirements vary from personal guarantees to letters of credit to hard assets, also depending upon lender and carrier requirements.

The terms of the loan and interest must be "reasonable," and there must be an exit strategy. Also, there must be a very high likelihood that the insured/owner will maintain coverage rather than sell it in the settlement market at a future date to recover the cost of premium financing or profit from a sale of the policy.

This type of financing may be acquired through an insured's personal bank, or through a lender that specializes in these types of loans.

Most carriers will accept traditional financing. However, there are some exceptions, either due to the terms of the loan or a general wariness about unfamiliar financing arrangements or specific lenders. It is best to check with a carrier prior to application submission to determine if they will accept the premium financing arrangement being proposed. If the arrangement is unfamiliar to the carrier, a due diligence process will likely ensue that examines the arrangement and whether it is suitable before coverage will be considered.

What type of financing arrangements are some carriers willing to consider that are more discretionary?

The discretionary financing arrangements come in several varieties and are commonly called "hybrids," since they have elements of several different financing methods. These are limited collateral arrangements and are typically short-term in duration. There are a few carriers that allow this type of financing arrangement as long as the applicant fact pattern is acceptable.

Common themes of hybrid financing plans are:

- The interest rate is tied to Libor or Prime, plus an additional 100 to 300 plus basis points of interest beyond these indices.
- Interest may or may not be rolled into the loan balance, depending upon lender and carrier requirements.
- The loan term ranges from 2 to 10 years. However, many carriers that consider these plans will only participate in a minimum 5-year loan arrangement
- Required collateral typically consists of the policy plus 10% to 25% additional collateral from the client – consisting of a personal guarantee, a letter of credit, or hard assets. The type and amount of collateral depends upon lender and carrier requirements. A third party medical evaluation on the proposed insured is typically required by the lender to determine "intrinsic" collateral value of the policy.

Similar to traditional premium financing, the applicant must have skin in the game. The terms of the loan and interest must be "reasonable." There must be a demonstrated need for coverage and a clearly articulated exit strategy once the financing period expires. Also, there must be a high likelihood that the owner will maintain coverage, rather than sell it at a future date to recover the cost of premium financing and/or profit from the sale of coverage by flipping it in the settlement market.

The carriers that participate in these arrangements may also have restrictions on the plan of coverage and face amounts they will issue.

What type of premium financing will the carriers not accept?

The carriers will absolutely not accept non-recourse premium financing and other similar financing schemes. This is IOLI/STOLI coverage where the applicant has no "skin in the game."

Because of the loan terms the applicant often turns the policy over to investors from whom they borrowed the money as satisfaction of their loan obligation. In these transactions, the applicants are often given inducements to enter into the loan by accepting free insurance, and/or upfront money that may sometimes be deferred for 2 years. Other times there may be an after-issue loan agreement, with a guaranteed letter of purchase.

This type of coverage has serious implications for the life industry. It is essentially a prearranged sale that turns life coverage into an investment vehicle for investors—which is not the true intent of life insurance. The tax-favored status afforded life insurance is one of the industry hallmarks that we all want to protect. No one wants or needs prearranged sales schemes that jeopardize the industry's future.

Non-recourse also has serious implications for applicants.

Besides the moral issues of investor-initiated coverage, it uses up the amount of available coverage they may qualify for and need in the future. It may also expose them to other things such as unknown and unwanted tax consequences.

What does an underwriter look at or need when underwriting premium finance coverage?

Almost all underwriters in the industry have expressed concern and frustration with underwriting coverage that is premium financed. At many carriers, the underwriters have been tasked as gatekeepers to make sure that they aren't taking coverage that may be IOLI/STOLI coverage in disguise. This has caused underwriters to be cautious and wary of any premium financing arrangements, no matter where business originates.

While carriers have made it easier for underwriters by providing approval to certain financing arrangements, some have not.

If an application disclosure is answered in a certain manner, or if there is something unusual about the fact pattern of an application (or a group of applications), the case is typically forwarded to a compliance area or a multi-organizational carrier team – typically consisting of underwriting, compliance, attorneys and others – that scrutinize the application more closely. This process can be frustrating for producers and underwriters since it can often take days or weeks to get feedback or acceptance of a particular financing arrangement.

If a case is being premium financed, the underwriters first and foremost look at two things:

1. Is THERE IS A LEGITIMATE LONG TERM LIFE INSURANCE OR ESTATE PLANNING NEED? If there is no need articulated, there is no coverage.

2. DOES THE SALE MAKE SENSE USING PREMIUM FINANCING? This is a broad question which may bring up a host of other questions and need for information. For example:

    • Term sheets to determine whether there is skin in the game, or to determine if loan terms are reasonable so the owner may keep the policy rather than having to sell it to pay off the debt.

- Loan agreement to indicate all debt obligations and who is financing the loan. This includes the promissory note, collateral assignment, loan disbursement information, grantor information, and an opinion letter from an attorney if necessary. The carriers want to be sure there are no hidden terms or agreements that may turn this into an IOLI/STOLI sale, or that all terms of the loan are reasonable and suggest a high likelihood the applicant will maintain coverage.
- Illustrations to look at premium funding requirements and subsequent borrowing that may occur.
- Trust documents if the trust was developed in the last 2 to 3 years to uncover such things as beneficial interests changes or similar language that may indicate the sale of coverage to investors or other third parties.
- Indications of a viable exit strategy other than death of the insured. An exit strategy is viewed by many carriers as an "acid test" to determine whether a premium financing arrangement is legitimate or not. They look for the type of exit strategy, assets/monies that will fund the strategy and when it will occur. Exit strategies can be quite complex, and may include such things as defective trusts, the sale of future assets, grantor retained annuity trusts (GRATs), estate tax assumptions, gifting rules, and growth of assets.
- Income verification and tax forms to determine whether the insured has the ability to pay premiums, especially when the loan period expires on hybrid premium financing plans.
- Third party verified financial statements listing all assets and liabilities, as well as supporting source documentation such as brokerage statements, addresses for real estate owned, etc.
- Information about whether there were any discussions about or intent for coverage to be sold. This is usually determined via application disclosures, inspection report information, applicant interviews, producer statements and other means. However, the fact that there was discussion about coverage being sold will not necessarily disqualify an applicant for cov-

erage. For example, as part of a financial advisor due diligence process, it is incumbent to disclose the full slate of options available to an applicant should they not need or want coverage at a later date. One of the potential options amongst others is the sale of a policy. The key point is that the insurance coverage is intended for a long term need and the likelihood of selling coverage, while an option, is low.

- Indication of whether upfront money was discussed as an inducement for the owner/insured to purchase life insurance coverage.
- Indication if a life expectancy (LE) or similar report was completed on the applicant. However, in and of itself, an LE does not disqualify an applicant for coverage, but it may cause additional questions to be asked. There are many valid reasons for doing an LE, including:

    - How long an applicant wants their guaranteed death benefit to stay in effect on a UL death benefit guaranteed plan of coverage. Coverage is less costly if the death benefit guarantee period is dialed down.
    - Estate planning techniques that consider timing and the applicant's estimated lifetime for the orderly transfer of estate assets to heirs.

As you can see, policing, requesting and following up on this information are a chore for anyone, especially your underwriter.

What things can you do to make things easier?

Given all the concerns about premium financing, your underwriter will err on the side of conservatism if not given well articulated reasons and explanations for what is being proposed.

It is critical to provide a well thought out and detailed cover memo highlighting the important aspects of your case and addressing any concerns your underwriter may have—upfront!

In addition to helping get your case approved, a cover memo will enhance your reputation as a producer who knows premium financing and how to do it correctly. Your underwriter will appreciate this and will give you the benefit of the doubt if there are questions.

Premium financed policies are typically in the hundreds of thousands in premium. **Don't leave anything to chance with these cases. Your income depends on it!**

CLOSING OBSERVATIONS

For many reasons, financial underwriting has gotten really tough over the last couple of years. Carriers are requesting more financial information than in the past and are underwriting this information closer, especially for large face amount applications, and especially those on older applicants. Because of this, it *pays* to take extra preparation time for financial underwriting prior to carrier submission of an application.

Here are a few key things to keep in mind as you put together a financial case for your underwriter:

- Be aware of the items underwriters consider when financially underwriting an application and what they view as important. Think about what the underwriter should know about your applicant and what information they gather. Address concerns and issues upfront.
- While each carrier is similar in their financial underwriting approach, there are also differences. Be aware of the criteria and formula used by the various carriers when financially underwriting a case, and provide an explanation for anything that deviates from published criteria.
- Underwriters consider the source of business when financially underwriting cases. If you establish yourself as a solid financial producer who knows your stuff, your underwriter will find ways to make your life easier and will often be more liberal when

financially underwriting your cases.

- When considering premium finance coverage, be sure to clearly articulate the applicant's long term life insurance and estate planning need, and why premium financing makes sense. Make sure there is an exit strategy as well.
- Always, always prepare memos in large case submissions. Don't leave your six figure commissionable income to chance on something that will take a few minutes to explain to your underwriter in a cover memo.

It only takes minutes to do financial underwriting properly.

Take the time and prepare for the best results.

CHAPTER 13

—————•————•————•————•—————

Topics in Medical Underwriting

This final section of the book examines some of the more important issues in medical underwriting. The focus is on contemporary issues and how they do – or should – influence underwriting now and in the years ahead.

CORONARY ARTERY DISEASE (CAD)

What is coronary artery disease?

The (usually) progressive development of atherosclerotic plaque lesions within the arteries, which gradually narrows their diameter and thereby reduces blood flow to the heart muscle.

When this flow is substantially impaired, the individual may develop chest pains and related symptoms which we call angina pectoris. If these plaque lesions rupture, the result will be an acute coronary event. This is known as acute coronary syndrome (ACS), which may present as a myocardial infarction (heart attack) or a similar but less severe condition called unstable angina pectoris.

How has our view on CAD changed over the last decade?

We used to see CAD as a "plumbing" problem, focusing on the extent of artery blockages more or less in a vacuum. Now we know that the critical factor is whether or not the plaque lesions are unstable. Unlike stable calcified plaque, unstable plaque is prone to rupture. This explains why some people – with stable plaque – live for years, even decades, with CAD and never have a coronary event while others – even with minimal and non-obstructive plaque – have a heart attack.

Has this revelation changed the way physicians manage CAD?

Yes.

The number of cases treated surgically, especially with coronary artery bypass, has declined, while the use of medication (in lieu of surgery) has increased. We have excellent pharmaceuticals for this purpose now, which were not available in the past.

There has also been an increased emphasis on secondary prevention. This means interventions to reduce the risk of coronary events in patients with known CAD before they occur.

Lipid-lowering drugs, mainly the so-called "statins," have been shown to delay or impede progression of CAD, and even reverse the process to some extent. These and others medications substantially reduce the risk of heart attacks even when obstructive plaque is present.

Has this changed CAD underwriting?

Yes, in a number of ways:

- We have liberalized our underwriting of best cases of chronic stable angina.
- We are paying more attention to the presence and severity of risk factors predisposing to vulnerable plaque, and less solely to the degree of obstruction (as demonstrated by coronary angiography)

in a vacuum.

- Evidence of atherosclerotic problems at other key sites such as the circulation to the brain and lower extremities is being factored into our assessments. This is done because of the synergistic effects of clinically significant multisite atherosclerotic disease.

- We are more aggressively underwriting surgically treated CAD where key parameters predicting for survival are favorable. One of these is the amount of blood pumped from the left ventricle when the heart contracts, known as the LV ejection fraction (LVEF). There are a number of others as well.

- Heart attack survivors are not only being scrutinized for residual cardiac damage, but also in terms of such things as the level of the heart attack marker troponin at the time of the event as well as afterwards, along with a variety of other risk factors predisposing to further events.

- Increasing emphasis is being placed on whether or not smokers quit or continue, patient compliance with physician advice, adherence to taking prescribed Rx, whether or not depression is present and the life circumstances of the subject (is he socially isolated, for example), together with the results of tests for inflammation, anemia…and insidious heart abnormalities which may not be producing symptoms as yet.

How can we increase our chances of getting a favorable offer on CAD cases?

The more information we have related to the above-mentioned considerations, the greater our latitude in what we can offer.

Teleinterviews get at matters which may not be addressed in an APS. Therefore, your odds are enhanced considerably when one of these interviews is done. The same is true for an Rx profile, which tells us a great deal about medication aspects of the risk, especially whether or not the applicant is compliant.

When the NT-proBNP test is done, and the results are normal, this is powerful evidence for a lack of residual heart damage. Hopefully, it won't be long before this unique test is performed routinely on all CAD cases.

If comorbidities (additional impairments) are present – which is the rule in older age CAD patients – the emphasis will be on how they relate to the risk of first-time or repeat cardiac events. Current kidney function status, for example, is quite important in the context of CAD. The same is true for control of blood sugar in diabetics with CAD.

Contrary to widely held superstition, it is to the client's advantage for the underwriter to have as much information as possible. All too often, it's what we don't know that raises underwriters' "antennae" and leads to conservative decision-making.

DIABETES

How important is diabetes in terms of mortality and morbidity?

More important than most producers realize!

In most studies of older-age subjects, diabetes retains a highly significant risk impact even at ages 70 and over.

While the relative impact of many other traditional mortality risk factors may dwindle to the point of irrelevance in the elderly, diabetes continues to have adverse implications, even more so when it is inadequately controlled or fraught with complications.

What are the most important considerations when we underwrite a diabetic?

- Is the applicant's blood sugar under control? Evidence for this comes from the applicant when we do teleinterviews, but is mainly driven by lab tests we routinely order, as well as what is revealed in the APS.

- Is he compliant with his physician's instructions, as well as in taking his Rx?
- Does he see his physician often enough to ensure adequate surveillance of his diabetic state?
- Does he have diabetic complications, including kidney damage, advanced eye disease, nerve involvement or foot problems, or anything indicative of circulatory disease?

Aren't the type of diabetes and the duration of the disease as important as the considerations just cited?

In our view, no – which is not to say that it doesn't matter at all if the person has type 1 rather than type 2 diabetes, or whether he has been diabetic for 5 years as compared to quarter of a century!

Type 1 diabetics are generally diagnosed at a much younger age than most type 2's. Therefore, at any given attained age, they have likely had more time to develop complications. But it is whether or not they have done so that drives the mortality and morbidity risk...rather than duration of disease in a vacuum.

In most cases, type 2 diabetes' onset is gradual. Many will have been told they have either or both forms of prediabetes – impaired fasting glucose (IFG) and impaired glucose tolerance (IGT) – for a period of time before they are diagnosed as fully diabetic.

Nevertheless, in terms of insurance risk, it is not so much how long one has been a diabetic as it is whether one has well-controlled blood sugar and/or any diabetic complications.

What are the things we look at closely when reviewing current studies and medical records on diabetics?

- Do recent and current blood sugar and glycosylated hemoglobin (HbA1-c) readings reflect adequate control of blood sugar?
- Does the applicant monitor control at home and, if so, what can

he tell us about the results of home tests?

- Is control being sustained without resorting to additional medications or increased doses of insulin?
- If he is type 2, is he obese? If so, has he achieved and sustained any significant degree of weight loss?
- Has the attending physician recently examined his eyes? Does he have any degree of retinopathy (retinal damage) and if so how extensive is this? Does he have cataracts, glaucoma or any other vision-related disease?
- Are his kidney-related tests within normal limits?
- Has he had and/or does he currently have albumin (protein) in his urine, and if so to what degree?
- Has he had signs or symptoms of diabetic nerve disease?
- Has he practiced proper diabetic foot care? Has he had any foot issues related to diabetes and if so how serious have they been?
- Are there any abnormalities in his CV risk profile and, if so, which ones and how severe are they?
- Has he had circulatory disease symptoms?
- Impaired circulation to the lower extremities is especially important in diabetics. The best test for early pathology is the ankle:brachial index (ABI), which is a comparison of blood pressure in the legs to that in the arms. Has this test been done and if so what are the results?
- Does he have any ECG abnormalities?

Hopefully you see from the extent of this list of issues how thorough we are when underwriting diabetics.

What can producers do to expedite the assessment of diabetic clients?

Help us get the answers to these questions!

Understand that just as adverse findings often make the risk worse, favorable ones allow us greater latitude to underwrite more liberally.

In my experience, favorable factors in cases of chronic disease are too often overshadowed by details related to adversities. One way this can be brought into balance is with the teleinterview. A properly configured drilldown questionnaire on diabetes will get at all of this and more.

Cancer

What is currently the #1 issue in cancer underwriting?

Insurers are concerned by the number of cancer death claims incurred within the time the first few policies are in force. These are usually cases which looked like good risks, free of anything consistent with a near-term cancer diagnosis.

What could explain this phenomenon?

- Some types of cancer are prone to be first diagnosed when they are far advanced. One of these is carcinoma of the pancreas, and the incidence of pancreatic cancer is rising.
- Other cancers are highly aggressive, often resulting in death within a year or two after they are diagnosed.
- Many early cancer-related symptoms are quite vague and are commonly encountered in benign conditions, which means we may not associate them with a high risk of undiagnosed cancer.
- Some of these early claims are clearly the result of antiselection, wherein the proposed insured bought the insurance either in the wake of new symptoms or after being given a cancer diagnosis.

What can underwriters do to pinpoint these cases?

- Pursue medical records when applicants report such things as worsening fatigue, suspicious headaches, a breast lump or enlarged lymph nodes which their primary care doctor dismissed as insignificant, and so on. The only downside of this is that it slows down the underwriting process. Thus, underwriters need to carefully select those cases where medical records are essential.

- Make teleinterviews universal, so that we optimize the amount of risk-related information. Teleinterviews facilitate accurate decision-making on recent symptoms, etc.
- Enhance underwriters' understanding of the often subtle clues to possible cancer which need to be resolved before the case is approved. This approach is so intrinsic to solving this problem that we have an entire 2009 Continuing Education course devoted to CLUES TO CANCER.
- Make greater use of appropriate cancer marker tests. The majority of insurers already screen at some age and amount threshold with PSA, the only tumor marker approved for general screening at this time. A few have been dabbling in other tumor markers, most notably CEA (carcinoembryonic antigen). We believe that using CEA in this manner is a recipe for disaster and we vigorously oppose its use in underwriting screening.

Has cancer mortality been improving in recent years?

Overall, it has not, mainly because there haven't been any major breakthroughs in treating metastatic malignancies arising in the most prevalent sites (lung, colon, breast, pancreas, etc.). This said, many encouraging studies are underway using new methods of treatment, and there is plenty of reason for optimism in the years ahead.

Most of the good news involves diagnosing cancer when it is still localized and amenable to cure. Clinical medicine has had considerable success in this regard, both from screening and from enhanced awareness of cancer warning signs by the general public.

How does this relate back to insurability?

We are seeing a higher percentage of cancers diagnosed "in situ," which means they are almost always cured by simple excision (surgical removal) and thus readily insurable (in some cases, by the time the stitches are removed!).

Take melanoma for example.

This cancer is seen often in underwriting because it often occurs in midlife, when the majority can be cured surgically (indeed, surgery is the only mode of treatment which is proven to be curative at this time).

Because of increasing rates of early detection, the majority of new cases of melanoma are either noninvasive (in situ) or still in a phase of growth seldom associated with metastases. This allows us to make far more liberal offers on recently diagnosed early melanoma than we could just five or ten years ago.

Are insurers also underwriting other kinds of cancer more aggressively?

You bet.

Two examples are illustrative:

PROSTATE CANCER

Because of widespread screening with PSA, the percentage of prostate cancers diagnosed when they have not spread beyond that organ has skyrocketed. While this has been happening, our understanding of the key factors predicting for silent spread (that is, where the disease has metastasized and is incurable, but there are not symptoms or findings associated with this process early on) has also increased dramatically.

We are seeing many cases which would once have been postponed for years but are now readily eligible for competitive offers. This is especially true at ages 70 and over, where prostate cancers can often be underwritten quite aggressively because of:

- The indolence of the disease process in many patients
- The potential for certain therapies to delay progression
- The general life expectancy of the applicant

In most of these cases it is fair to say that the individual will die "with" but not "of" this malignancy.

BREAST CANCER

Screening with mammograms has resulted in a huge increase in the percentage of breast carcinomas discovered when they are still "in situ," as well as invasive cancers being diagnosed when they are quite small.

Breast cancer in situ rarely spreads and is usually insurable soon after completion of treatment. The risk in most of these cases is additional breast tumors, some of which may turn out to be invasive.

Therefore, the two main concerns in women successfully treated for breast cancer in situ are:

- Their overall breast cancer risk (based on the kind of in situ breast tumor, their family history and the age at diagnosis of the in situ cancer).
- Whether or not they are compliant with the enhanced degree of follow-up (more frequent MD visits, more mammograms and often additional tests such as MRIs or ultrasound) necessary to detect new tumors when they are still readily treatable.

We also know that there is a powerful correlation between the size of a breast cancer and its prognosis. This has motivated some pace-setting insurers to make more attractive offers on cases where the cancer is rather small.

What is the driver in cancer underwriting?

The quality of underwriting guidelines.

Cancer is the most challenging major disease we underwrite. There are over 200 major varieties and each has specific characteristics related to prognosis (and thus insurability). Therefore, the underwriting manual must be sufficiently comprehensive to ensure informed, competitive decision-making.

If I have a concern here, it is for adequacy of tumor-specific guidelines in underwriting manuals. I've seen too many cases where highly significant prognostic factors go unaddressed because underwriting practices have not been adjusted for important developments (and in some cases they are not all that recently discovered!).

Maintaining underwriting guidelines at a high level of excellence is a daunting task that requires sufficient allocation of staff resources. This has been our Achilles' heel. Individuals who should be giving first priority to underwriting manual upgrading have been pushed into "production" instead.

Why has this been allowed to happen?

Because legitimate staffing needs are ignored.

What are the 6 things the underwriter must know to properly underwrite a cancer case?

- What was the PRECISE diagnosis? The importance of this cannot be overstated. What may seem, from your perspective, to be overly "picky" distinctions between two subtypes of a given tumor could wind up having more to do with insurability than all the other evidence combined!
- The pathology report. APS summarization efforts I've seen have largely been a bust in trying to accurately gauge what matters on these reports. One really needs considerable expertise before attempting to dissect pathology reports. And what is found here often drives the underwriting decision.
- The records of the attending physician. And if those records do not include sufficient detail about care provided by the oncologist, then quite likely an APS from the oncologist will be

pursued as well. Cancer is not an impairment where it is cost-effective to take a "lean and mean" approach to underwriting requirements!

- The interim (post-cancer treatment) history. Did the cancer ever recur and, if it did, where, when, and so on? Have there been any new, suspicious symptoms or findings which could herald either a recurrence or a delayed adverse effect from prior therapies?
- Patient compliance. There must be adequate follow-up as advised by the doctor(s) caring for the applicant. Follow-up M.D. visits and tests the applicant was advised to have, which have been put off for whatever reason, are RED FLAGS! As an underwriter, I wouldn't blink an eye at postponing a current application until the proposed insured took care of these important matters...and the results were in my hand.
- The current health status of the applicant.

Does the fact that cancer has metastasized (spread) mean the risk is always uninsurable?

There are some cancers where minimal spread, mainly to lymph nodes, does not wholly compromise insurability. Unfortunately, just the opposite is true in most cases where the cancer has metastasized.

What are the 3 main underwriting concerns in cases where the cancer has spread?

The 3 main ones are:

- **Where has it spread?**

  In papillary thyroid carcinoma, lymph node spread may not adversely affect mortality, with notable exceptions at older ages and certain subtypes of this tumor. If the pattern of lymph node spread in testicular seminoma is favorable, the same is true because of the high cure rate with radiation therapy.

- **HOW EXTENSIVELY HAS IT SPREAD?**

  When tumors metastasize extensively to lymph nodes beyond the immediate vicinity of the tumor or to internal organs like the liver, bones and brain, the prognosis is almost always so unfavorable that insurability is not a consideration.

- **HOW LONG HAS THE APPLICANT BEEN IN REMISSION (DEFINED AS OSTENSIBLY FREE OF CANCER) AFTER COMPLETION OF HIS TREATMENT?**

  The interval from completion of treatment for metastatic cancer and the point at which life insurance can be offered differs widely. Many cases of lung metastasis in testicular carcinoma will be insurable in just a few years. Conversely, the risk of recurrence and a fatal outcome with kidney cancer and melanoma is so great that few cases, even with protracted periods of survival, will be deemed insurable.

Most underwriting manuals don't go into any depth on this subject. Therefore, making the best decision often involves doing considerable research in the medical literature.

Do the effects of cancer treatment ever impact insurability?

They should, but from what we have seen, the appreciation of this critical factor varies widely among insurers.

Both radiation and chemotherapy can exert profound adverse effects. Some are evident, and even fatal, during the treatment or in the short term after the therapy has been administered. These are not significant to us because of the inevitable waiting period before we make an offer.

Long-term treatment-related adversities, on the other hand, must be a major consideration in underwriting. These delayed effects may present in 3 ways:

- **Second tumors**

  Radiation and some anticancer drugs are carcinogenic, resulting in extra risk for developing new cancers. The magnitude of this depends upon the specific form of treatment, how much was given and the interval since completion of treatment. Chemotherapy-induced new tumors tend to occur far sooner than those incited by radiation.

- **Organ damage**

  Certain chemotherapy drugs are irreversibly damaging to the heart and other organs, especially if larger doses are given. In the case of the heart, such damage is often silent (free of symptoms or suspicious test findings) for many years and may only become apparent when it interacts with other mechanisms of heart damage such as high blood pressure or atherosclerosis. Radiation damage may also cause chronic organ malfunction and, in the case of the heart, work synergistically with chemotherapy-induced damage.

- **Functional difficulties**

  Radiation therapy directed to the brain may adversely affect physical growth and intellectual development in children. Chemotherapy is also a potential culprit here.

Bottom line: there are some cases involving readily insurable malignancies such as Hodgkin lymphoma where the cancer is deemed to be cured but the long-term risks of treatment-induced problems justifies a permanent rating. Typically that rating is fairly modest (one or two tables).

CHRONIC HEPATITIS C

What is chronic hepatitis C?

Infection with the hepatitis C virus which is not eradicated by the host's immune system and persists for 6 months or longer.

Do most cases of hepatitis become chronic?

Yes. Roughly 80%.

Is hepatitis C a prevalent cause of death?

Yes. It's now the 10th leading cause of death in the United States.

Which applicants are at significant risk of chronic hepatitis C?

This is important because symptoms of chronic hepatitis C typically do not emerge for several decades and hence a significant proportion of infected persons don't know they have the virus:

- Having had a blood transfusion prior to 1992 (which was when the test for hepatitis C started being used to screen blood donors).
- Intravenous drug use, currently or at any time in the past.
- Intranasal use (snorting) of cocaine and other drugs.
- Treatment for hemophilia or kidney dialysis in the past.
- History of sexually transmitted disease.
- Having tattoos, primarily depending on the sanitary practices (or lack thereof) of the place where the tattoo was administered.

How are most cases of chronic hepatitis C discovered?

Routine screening with a blood profile. The test most likely to be abnormal is the ALT liver enzyme.

How is the diagnosis made?

The first step in testing persons at increased risk, whether based on medical history or an elevated ALT level, is with the hepatitis C antibody test. This tells us if the person was ever infected but doesn't discriminate between persons who cleared the infection versus those who are still carrying the virus.

When the antibody test is positive (abnormal), we do an antigen test which directly detects the virus. If this is also positive, we know chronic hepatitis C is present.

How is the extent of liver damage determined?

Some infected persons do not have any abnormal liver tests. In most cases, this scenario is associated with a lower probability of liver damage, as compared to when one or more liver tests are elevated. If liver disease is suspected based on lab tests and/or findings on a physical examination, the doctor may order a hepatic (liver) ultra-sound test which uses sound waves to create a virtual picture of the liver. This test is very efficient at detecting liver damage.

The only test which can confirm the nature and extent of liver pathology is a liver biopsy. We rely greatly on the results of the liver biopsy, when one was done, in determining if the individual is insurable and, if so, at what rating.

Can chronic hepatitis C be treated?

Yes, usually with one or two drugs.

There are at least 6 major subtypes – called genotypes – of chronic hepatitis C and, depending upon which type the person has, the probability of effective treatment ranges from 40% to 80%+.

What are the important consequences of chronic hepatitis C?

In some affected persons, liver damage progresses at a steady rate, culminating in cirrhosis. Cirrhosis is often fatal and it also greatly increases the risk of liver cancer.

Chronic hepatitis C is also associated with a substantially increased risk of type 2 diabetes, and there are other potential non-liver related complications as well.

Is chronic hepatitis C ever insurable without a rating?

The answer, of course, depends on the carrier's underwriting philosophy.

If the best cases – based on all aspects of the history – are successfully treated before cirrhosis develops and in the absence of non-liver related issues, most experts would argue that there is little extra mortality risk …and what risk there may be in some of them is unlikely to become apparent for decades.

Determining which cases qualify on this basis is no easy task because so many considerations are involved.

Which factors are consistent with a BEST CASE?

In my course on chronic hepatitis C for underwriters, I identified over 20 factors worthy of consideration in this context. The top 8 are:

- Age of the applicant – most mortality risk is in persons age 50 and over.
- How the applicant became infected – which relates to the amount of virus entering the body.
- Favorable findings on liver biopsies – if more than one was done, we need to see them all because liver damage may wax and wane.
- Normal liver enzymes and especially no elevation of GGT.
- If the applicant was treated – sustained remission with no evidence of persistent viral infection.
- No important complications.
- Insured must be an alcohol abstainer or, at most, a very light user of alcoholic beverages. Robust alcohol consumption works

synergistically with hepatitis C infection to cause progressive liver damage.

- Normal cholesterol level – very low or falling cholesterol is highly unfavorable.

Psychiatric Disorders

How many psychiatric disorders are there?

Well over 100, but many are seldom seen in underwriting.

Where do we find the criteria for the diagnosis of these disorders?

In the USA, we use the Diagnostic and Statistical Manual of Mental Disorders, the current – that is, in 2008 – edition of which is known as DSM-IV-TR. The experts are working on DSM-V at this writing.

Elsewhere, the International Classification of Disease coding system (ICD-10) is the predominant source.

What is the #1 problem we encounter in psychiatric cases?

Getting enough information to accurately assess insurability!

Insurance applicants are uncomfortable disclosing information about psychiatric problems. This discomfort is apt to be most acutely experienced when the necessary questions are asked by their insurance agent.

It's almost as difficult to get candid answers on paramedical and medical exams. And we even have the same problem with medical records. Where psychiatric histories are concerned, they tend to be less informative, compared to any other major impairment.

For these reasons, the teleinterview is by far the best method of taking psychiatric medical histories. Trust me on this: it is to your client's advantage when his psychiatric history is taken during a teleinterview…

…because the more we know about these impairments, the better the odds of a favorable offer!

Why?

Because the less information the underwriter has about a significant psychiatric condition, the more likely he is to underwrite conservatively.

Is there significant extra mortality in psychiatric disorders?

It depends on which disorder, and in those which do pose a significant mortality risk, the whole case context. The leading cause of excess mortality in psychiatric disorders is suicide.

Which of the more common psychiatric disorders are associated with extra mortality?

Simply listing these impairments doesn't get to the key issues related to mortality risk. All it tells us is that some psychiatric conditions are more likely than others to have such issues present.

With this essential caveat, these are the disorders more likely to harbor excess mortality:

- Major depressive disorder (MDD)
- Bipolar disorder (BD)
- Alcohol abuse and dependency
- Drug abuse and dependency
- Schizophrenia and other forms of chronic psychosis
- Cognitive dysfunction and overt dementia
- Anorexia nervosa
- Antisocial personality disorder

- Borderline personality disorder

Do anxiety disorders have extra mortality?

As a rule, no – most of the risk involves morbidity.

However, there are some cases – usually those which are most severe and persistent – which do have increased mortality. In most of these, a second psychiatric diagnosis is often involved, either concurrently or in the past.

What are the key factors impacting our assessment of all psychiatric risks?

- Comorbidities.

  "Comorbidity" is the term we use for a coexisting disorder. Most persons with one psychiatric diagnosis have – or would be found to have if fully evaluated – at least one additional psychiatric condition.

  The more psychiatric disorders present, the higher the probability that one or more of these other risk factors below will come into play and thereby impact underwriting.

- History of suicidality.

  We don't mean only prior suicide attempts. The term "suicidality" also encompasses suicidal gestures (non-life-threatening acts symbolizing thoughts of self-harm) and suicidal ideation (habitually thinking about taking one's own life).

- Inpatient treatment.

  More severe disorders are treated on an inpatient basis, mostly in a psychiatric care facility.

- History of substance abuse.

  There is a strong link between substance abuse and both chronicity and suicidality in psychiatric disorders.

- Current heavy alcohol intake.
- Current use of drugs of abuse.
- Frequency and duration of relapses.
- Treatment with multiple medications – depending on which medications and how long they are needed.
- Treatment with certain highly potent medications at any time.
- Treatment with electroconvulsive therapy (electroshock) or certain other interventions.
- Psychotic features in nonpsychotic disorders.

Do coexisting psychiatric disorders impact the risk associated with medical disorders?

Potentially, depending on which psychiatric impairment is involved.

For example, many studies now show that survivors of heart attacks who are depressed have a substantially less favorable prognosis for overall survival as compared to those free of depression. This is true even if the depressive disorder itself is not serious enough to be debited on its own merits.

ALCOHOL ABUSE AND ALCOHOLISM

What is the difference between alcohol abuse and alcoholism?

Alcohol abuse means drinking too much, either daily or under specific circumstances.

Alcoholism means being dependent on alcohol, whether or not one is currently drinking.

While most heavy drinkers are never diagnosed with alcoholism, this fact does precious little to lessen their formidable mortality and morbidity implications.

What is considered heavy drinking?

Most experts set the threshold for abusive drinking at 80 grams or more of daily alcohol consumption in a man and 40 grams or more in a woman.

At ages 65 and over, these levels are reduced by 50%.

How do grams per day translate into drinks per day?

It depends on the amount of alcohol in the drink! A double scotch is going to have a lot more alcohol in it than a bottle of light beer!

Generally speaking, 80 grams is equivalent to between 4 and 6 drinks.

Thus, a man consuming > 4 drinks a day or a woman having > 2 drinks daily would meet most criteria for being a heavy drinker.

At older ages, > 2 drinks/day in a man or > 1 drink/day in a woman is considered too much.

What is binge drinking?

Consuming 5 or more drinks on one occasion.

Even though some bingers don't consume as much total alcohol as daily heavy drinkers, their risk is generally more unfavorable if only because of their increased risk of accidents in an intoxicated state.

What are the 2 main mortality-related consequences of heavy drinking?

* Accidental death

- Alcohol-induced disease

Does alcohol-induced disease pertain mainly to the liver?

No – sustained heavy drinking can have major consequences, directly or indirectly, for almost every bodily system.

In terms of liver disease, most heavy drinkers will develop a fatty liver (alcohol-induced steatosis). This condition usually has no symptoms and will typically regress if the person stops drinking. The other alcoholic liver disorders, which occur in only about 1 in 5 long-time heavy drinkers, are alcoholic hepatitis and alcoholic cirrhosis. Both of these have very high mortality.

What factors do underwriters consider in cases of alcohol abuse?

- How much the person drinks.
- The age at which he began to drink.
- How long he has been drinking heavily.
- How long since he either stopped or significantly reduced his drinking.
- The pattern of his drinking: daily vs. binge.
- Any evidence consistent with current or recent heavy drinking as reflected in laboratory tests done for underwriting or in his medical history.
- Family history of alcoholism or suicide in parents and siblings.
- His driving record, both alcohol-related and non-alcohol-related violations.
- Occupational, marital, social or legal problems due to drinking.
- Evidence of other substance abuse.
- Organ system pathology associated with heavy drinking.
- The presence of psychiatric comorbidities.

In other words, we underwrite alcohol abuse VERY thoroughly.

Are the same issues considered in applicants with a history of alcohol dependency (alcoholism)?

Yes.

In addition, we must address:

- When he was diagnosed with alcohol dependency.
- How he was treated.
- Whether there is any ongoing medical treatment and if so what that treatment is.
- Any relapses.
- When he attained sobriety and how long he has been continuously sober.
- Participation in AA or similar 12-step programs.

What if a recovered alcoholic is currently engaged in "controlled" drinking?

This is a hotly debated subject among experts in the field.

I take a conservative posture in this context because I can't envision a credible way, in an underwriting context, of distinguishing between "controlled drinking" vs. excessive drinking or relapse to abuse/dependency.

How long before a recovered alcoholic can qualify for life insurance?

There is considerable variation in underwriting practices. Understand that no two cases are ever alike and the final determination of the appropriate interval from recovery to insurability depends on all the facts of the case.

Broadly speaking, I have seen the very best cases accepted on some basis as early as 2-3 years after attainment of sustained sobriety. The average interval, on the other hand, is probably around 5 years.

Is drug abuse underwritten much the same as in alcohol abuse and alcoholism?

Yes.

Just as in alcohol abuse, drug abuse and drug dependency are distinct, and our approach to them is very similar to what we do where alcohol is the issue.

The biggest difference is the drug in question.

Some drugs lead to more serious health consequences than others. Therefore, we may take a more liberal approach to, for example, marijuana abuse than to heroin or cocaine abuse.

How widespread is drug use?

A recent federal government agency reports that 20.4 million Americans age 12 and older used an illicit drug within the last month.

A 2002 study of global drug use reported that 20 million North Americans used marijuana in the past 12 months. For cocaine, they cited 6.3 million for the USA and Canada combined.

It is further estimated that more than 1 in 3 Americans have tried marijuana at least one time.

Is marijuana use associated with extra mortality?

No doubt there are mortality implications associated with very heavy use. However, a study in Oakland, California, found no significant increase in mortality among past or current users.

What is the #1 underwriting concern with marijuana use?

If they use marijuana, what other drugs do they use?

Polydrug (2 or more drugs) abuse is so prevalent that we know a significant minority of "pot" smokers must use other illicit drugs and/ or excessive amounts of alcohol.

Another, albeit lesser (in my view) consideration is that marijuana is illegal in most places, so there is some concern about the kind of people one has to associate with to procure it.

How do insurers approach marijuana use?

Past use – assuming no abuse of other drugs, no complications and no known health consequences – is rarely if ever an issue, nor should it be.

Suffice it to say that there is no overall consensus on current use. Much depends on the individual circumstances and case context.

For example, one could argue that occasional use by an adult, in the absence of any other evidence of substance abuse or associated adversities, would not confer any significant extra risk. That is, of course, aside from the fact that nearly all marijuana users smoke the drug and marijuana smoke contains more or less the same toxins as cigarette smoke.

In an informal survey I conducted a couple of years ago, 86% of responding companies said they handled the typical case of current marijuana smoking on more or less the same basis as current cigarette smoking.

Why is our underwriting approach to cocaine much more conservative?

> *"Approximately 1 in every 4 nonfatal MIs* [heart attacks] *in persons aged 18 to 45 was attributable to frequent cocaine use."*
>
> Adrian Qureshi et al.
> Third National Health and Nutrition Survey
> *Circulation*
> 103(2001):502

Cocaine has a host of serious medical consequences which simply do not occur as a consequence of the equivalent use of marijuana.

To make matters worse, in the presence of cocaine and alcohol, the liver metabolizes the cocaine into a far more risky substance called cocaethylene.

Hence, the combination of heavy drinking plus cocaine ingestion is far riskier than using either substance separately.

Can we predict which cocaine users will suffer life-threatening consequences?

No.

Sometimes a single dose will be fatal while others will snort cocaine for years before they go "one snort over the line," so to speak.

Is methamphetamine use as significant to insurability as cocaine use?

Not merely "as significant" but actually more so because meth users are:

- More likely to be daily/heavy users (it's cheaper and more addicting!)
- More exposed to contaminants, considering how it is "manufactured"
- More likely to require treatment for abuse/addiction
- At even greater risk for serious medical complications
- More likely to have coexisting psychiatric disorders

Is the use of methamphetamine increasing?

Yes, whereas the use of cocaine is declining.

Which explains why some insurers are making use of methamphetamine screening in life underwriting.

MEDICAL UNDERWRITING IN THE ELDERLY

What needs to be done in older-age underwriting?

> *"For life insurance, all the demographics suggest that consumers age 65 and over make up a robust market, especially those who have money to spend. The key will be developing proper risk selection procedures, tests and protocols, along with the necessary risk management."*

> David M. Holland, FSA, MAAA
> President, Munich American Re
> LOMA *Resource*
> January 2007

Bulls-eye, Dave! You hit the nail on the head.

When I work with new underwriters on this subject, the first thing I tell them is to forget everything they thought they knew…because so many of the "rules" must change in order to accommodate the realities of geriatric risks.

What is considered "older age" for underwriting purposes?

We have a problem here now because we tend to use "geriatric," "older age" and "elderly" interchangeably, and these terms are apt to be defined in many different ways, depending on one's perspective.

In the past, most companies considered age 65 the threshold for "older age."

Today, I think most of my peers would agree that the "elderly" threshold has shifted to age 70.

What is the #1 difference between how we underwrite persons at ages 41-69 as compared to when they are age 70 and older?

In the younger group, we focus on chronic disease.

In the elderly, the emphasis shifts to physical frailty and cognitive function. This does not mean that chronic diseases cease to matter, but rather that we know their risk of succumbing to chronic disease is greatly impacted by frailty and cognition.

Study after study has shown that markers for frailty and cognitive function have a stronger association with excess mortality and morbidity than virtually all of the factors that matter to us, as underwriters, in younger applicants.

What are the benchmarks for cognitive dysfunction and premature physical frailty?

We have three aggregations of markers related to frailty and cognitive function:

- Cognitive function markers
- Direct and indirect frailty markers
- Vulnerability markers

Which cognitive function markers do insurers use when examining elderly applicants?

The top four are:

- Delayed word recall
- Clock drawing
- Mini-Mental Status Exam (MMSE)
- Short Portable Mental Status Questionnaire (SPMSQ)

What are the direct and indirect frailty markers?

Many direct tests for frailty have come into use both clinically and in insurance screening. The more widely used ones include how long it takes to either rise from a chair or walk a measured distance.

On the indirect side, we have both the activities of daily living (ADLs) and the instrument activities of daily living (IADLs). They address a diversity of performance-related issues inexorably associated with the capacity for daily functioning and independent living.

Do all life insurers use these tests?

No…well, not yet anyway.

Two years ago only 1 in 5 routinely required cognitive and frailty testing. However, their use continues to rise and I have no doubt they will be required more or less universally, albeit at differing age thresholds and face amounts, in the near-term future.

At what age do insurers begin using frailty and cognitive markers?

In the 2007 Underwriting Requirements Survey:

- 25% start under age 70
- 21% begin at age 70
- 21% initiate these tests between ages 71 and 74
- 12% commence at age 75
- 21% don't require them until after age 75

At what face amount threshold are these tests required?

Here again, practices range, literally, from "over $1,000,000" to "all cases." These thresholds are driven, at least in part, by the average face amounts written by the carrier in this market.

Are these cognitive and frailty tests done mainly on medical examinations?

No. Six out of 10 companies require them on paramedicals and 40% use them only on M.D. exams.

Are cognitive and frailty questions asked during teleinterviews?

Yes.

In the 2007 survey, 22% of insurers asked cognitive questions and 35% included frailty-related questions (mainly ADLs) in their teleinterviews in the elderly applicant population.

What are the key vulnerability markers?

In my view, these are the four which matter most:

- Underweight/weight loss
- Low or falling cholesterol
- Low or falling serum albumin
- Pack-years of cigarette smoking

What defines underweight?

I prefer to use body mass index (BMI), as opposed to build tables. Based on BMI, a reading < 18.5 is consistent with underweight in this context.

Why do we place more emphasis on underweight in the elderly?

Because studies show that the extra mortality of underweight is relatively greater in the elderly than it is at younger ages.

Is underweight more significant than overweight and obesity in the elderly?

Absolutely...well, at least until you get well into stage 2 obesity, defined as a body mass index (BMI) between 35 and 39.9.

Which is more significant in the elderly: underweight or weight loss?

Weight loss, when:

- The cause is unknown or the explanation given is dubious

- The amount lost is ≥ 5% of that individual's weight at the time the loss began

What constitutes "low" cholesterol?

Various thresholds have been cited in clinical studies, ranging from 160 mg/dL or less to 120 mg/dL and under. I tend to use 140 mg/dL as my "cut point" for calling someone's cholesterol too low.

Does this pertain if someone has always had low cholesterol at that level or below?

No, not when we have medical records that clearly establish a history of stable low readings for at least 5 years and no other red flags are present.

What if the applicant's cholesterol is very low because of aggressive medical treatment of high cholesterol?

This is a much-debated issue in clinical medicine. Some say "the lower, the better." Others are more cautious, expressing concern for pushing the cholesterol so low that there isn't enough of it left to perform its necessary bodily functions.

You don't see a whole lot of elderly patients whose cholesterol is under 140 due to treatment. But when it does happen, case context drives my handling of the cholesterol reading.

Which matters more: low cholesterol or falling cholesterol?

Falling cholesterol, provided the applicant is not on treatment for high cholesterol or taking some other drug that could induce this effect.

Like weight loss, significantly falling cholesterol (in the absence of treatment to induce it) is an insidious indicator of either worsening chronic disease or some as-yet undiscovered new illness.

Why does serum (blood) albumin come into the picture here?

Because it is the best blood profile marker for frailty.

There is extra mortality associated with any degree of hypo-albuminemia (low blood albumin) and it gets worse if the level is falling over periodic measurements.

What defines a pack-year of smoking?

As we said earlier, if you smoke one pack (20 cigarettes) per day for one year, you accumulate a dose equal to one pack-year. If you smoke 10 per day instead, it takes 2 years to get one pack-year. On the other hand, if you smoke 2 packs daily, at the end of one calendar year you will have 2 pack-years of exposure.

How does pack-years of cigarette smoking factor in here?

- Cigarette smoking is a risk factor for more diseases than any other single characteristic except aging.
- Most of the serious adverse effects of cigarette smoking are dose-related.
- Pack-years is the only effective way to measure total cigarette exposure.

Is there a threshold at which pack-years become significant independent of whether or not one happens to be currently smoking?

I'm sure there is. I just haven't delved deeply enough into the subject to tell you precisely what that level of pack-years is. Until I do so, I prefer to use 50 pack-years, having no doubt that allowing for this much exposure equates to a rather generous posture!

Once an applicant has reached 50 pack-years, I would never again allow him to qualify as a non-smoker even if he quits and stays quit. The damage has been done.

Are there any anticipated developments in underwriting screening which could change our approach to chronic disease risk in elderly applicants?

Yes...and we have already made reference to these elements earlier so we won't belabor the point!

Several potential screening tests now afford us an unprecedented opportunity to sort cardiovascular and all-cause mortality risks in this population:

- **NT-proBNP** – the finest screening test ever for circulatory impairment.
- **Hemoglobin A1-c (HbA1-c)** – the test used to assess control in diabetics which we now know also relates to the risk of CV disease in non-diabetics as well.
- **Hemoglobin** – a routine test in clinical medicine which has also been shown to relate directly to chronic disease risk and mortality in the elderly.
- **Cystatin C** – a promising new marker initially related to early kidney damage but now showing promise in other domains related to geriatric risk.

INDEX

———●———●———●———●———

C

M

N

O

HANK GEORGE

Hank George is one of six thousand (give or take) North Americans of vastly heterogenous backgrounds who discovered they had a gift for the art and science of life and health underwriting. He is a CLU, FLMI and, most importantly, a Fellow – with distinction – of the Academy of Life Underwriting (FALU).

Hank has been an underwriter for 36 years. He began his career with Northwestern Mutual and after one year stints with Manufacturer's Life and Lincoln National Re, joined Home Office Reference Laboratory (now ExamOne) in 1988. In 2003, he became self-employed in an all-family enterprise known as Hank George Inc. (HGI, for short).

Over these years, Hank founded *On The Risk* and served as its editor-in-chief for 18 years. He also launched the International Underwriting Congress in 1996 and chaired the IUC through its first four conferences. He currently writes periodic articles and essays for *The National Underwriter* and *Best's Review*, and has published over 300 books, papers, articles and essays.

Hank has addressed most of the world's major underwriting and life insurance sales organizations, including two main platform presentations at the Million Dollar Round Table (MDRT) as well as two lectures at the Top of the Table. He has organized nearly 100 educational events domestically and internationally, including over 40 seminars for the Society of Actuaries. He writes two e-newsletters: *Hot Notes,* a free monthly with 1,500+ readers around the globe and *JournalScan*, a bimonthly subscription-based medical underwriting periodical.

Hank resides in his home town (Milwaukee), is a devout Cheesehead and a relentless political blogger.

The main HGI website is www.hankgeorgeinc.com. Hank may be reached at hankgeorge@aol.com and (414)423-0967.

DuWayne Kilbo, MBA, FLMI

DuWayne is a Principal of Windsor Insurance Associates, Inc., a Brokerage General Agency based out of Woodland Hills, California. His background includes over 20 years of Home Office and field underwriting experience in the areas of underwriting strategy development and implementation, brokerage management, agent recruitment, reinsurance treaty development and negotiation, home office underwriting management, underwriting standard development, case underwriting, and process improvement.

DuWayne has also been a guest speaker for insurance industry groups on a variety of underwriting related topics and is a published author.

You may contact him at duwayne@windsorinsurance.com or 818-710-9890.